The Gift Of
SHABBAT

Unlocking The Eternal Rest That Changes Everything

Scott & Amanda Cumbee

CUMBEES.COM

CUMBEES HOUSE OF PUBLISHING

CUMBEES HOUSE of Torah and Worship

CUMBEES HOUSE of Publishing
A Wholly Owned Subsidiary of CUMBEES HOUSE
Whiteville, NC 28472
Cumbees.com

Copyright © 2025 by CUMBEES HOUSE, Scott Cumbee and Amanda Cumbee
All rights reserved.

No part of this book may be reproduced, stored in a retrieval system or transmitted in any form or by any means electronic, mechanical, photocopy, recording or otherwise without the prior written permission of the publisher, except in the case of brief quotations embodied in critical articles or reviews.

ISBN: 979-8-9930517-0-3 (Hardback)
ISBN: 979-8-9930517-1-0 (Paperback)
ISBN: 979-8-9930517-2-7 (eBook)
ISBN: 979-8-9930517-3-4 (Audio)

Library of Congress Control Number: 2025919282

Printed in the United States of America
10 9 8 7 6 5 4 3 2 1

Some Scripture quotations are from the King James Version (KJV), with the name of God such as LORD restored to [*YeHoVaH*] or [*YHVH*] and Jesus to [*Yeshua*]. Also, The Holy Spirit restored to [*Ruach HaKodesh*] and law to [*Torah*].

This Book is Presented in Love and Faith

*To:*_____

*From:*_____

*Date:*_____

A gift of love, faith and truth to encourage your journey.

"Thy word is a lamp unto my feet, and a light unto my path" (**Psalm 119:105** KJV).

*Note:*_____
_____
_____
_____
_____
_____
_____
_____
_____
_____
_____

Bible Copyright Notices

Amplified Bible (AMP):
Scripture quotations taken from the Amplified® Bible, copyright © 2015 by The Lockman Foundation. Used by permission. www.lockman.org All rights reserved.

Complete Jewish Bible (CJB):
Scripture quotations taken from the Complete Jewish Bible, copyright © 1998 and 2016 by David H. Stern. Used by permission of Messianic Jewish Publishers, www.messianicjewish.net. All rights reserved worldwide.

English Standard Version (ESV):
Scripture quotations are from the ESV® Bible (The Holy Bible, English Standard Version®), copyright © 2001 by Crossway, a publishing ministry of Good News Publishers. Used by permission. www.esv.org All rights reserved.

Hebrew Translation Version (HTV):
Scripture quotations taken from The Hebrew Book of Matthew copyright © 2025 by Miles R. Jones. Used by permission. www.writingofgod.com All rights reserved.

King James Version (KJV):
Public Domain.

The Mark Biltz Bible (MBB):
Scripture quotations taken from the Mark Biltz Bible copyright © 2025 by Mark Biltz and Dr. Danny Ben Gigi Used by permission. www.esm.us All rights reserved.

World English Bible (WEB):
Public Domain

Table of Contents

Forward 6
Dedication 11
In Loving Memory and Honor of the Faithful 13
A Call to Prepare Your Heart 14
Introduction 18
1. The Verdict of Eternity: Torah and Shabbat Still Stand 23
2. The Unbroken Covenant: Shabbat and His Commandments Still Stand 34
3. The Origin and Covenant of the Sabbath: A Gift from the Beginning 37
4. The Spiritual Covenant of Shabbat: A Prophetic Foretaste of Eternity 41
5. Preparing for Shabbat: Welcoming the King with Joy 51
6. Welcoming the Sabbath: Entering His Rest with Light and Blessing 59
7. The Flow of Shabbat: A Day of Worship, Rest and Renewal 84
8. Havdalah: Carrying the Light into the Week 90
9. The Book of Remembrance: When Covenant Is Recorded in Heaven 95
10. The Secret Place: Dwelling in the Shadow of the Almighty 99
11. The Cost of Covenant: Death for Life 105
12. Shabbat Eternal: Rest, Warning and the Call to Covenant 120
13. Shabbat: Heaven's Wedding Rehearsal 125
14. Covenant Practices and Explanations 132
15. 52-Week Torah Reading Cycle with Prophets & New Covenant Parallels . 139
16. Shabbat: The Covenant of the Bride 147

Forward

Scott and Amanda have done a masterful job in laying out not only the Scriptural reasons for keeping and honoring the Sabbath; they also deliver to the reader the very heart of the Sabbath! Everyone knows life is always about relationships. At Creation God created everything mankind would need to survive and thrive.

As always, the best is saved for last; God knew that mankind needed a day set aside to build a personal relationship with Him.

I thank Scott and Amanda for all their hard work and their deep dive into the Sabbath and their hearts desire to make all believers understand the depth that they can achieve by honoring what the King of the Universe has requested of His kids!

Blessings!

Mark Biltz

Pastor Mark Biltz
El Shaddai Ministries
Office 253-862-8010
www.esm.us

I have known Scott & Amanda Cumbee for years and their genuine and humble zeal for the Lord, as well as their love for Him, is what I believe helped birth their new book, *The Gift of Shabbat*. This book will definitely be an eye-opener to everyone who picks it up to read it. Not only that, but you will learn things you've never known about God's Holy feasts.

Scott and Amanda take their walk with the Lord very seriously and their fruit has poured out on these pages. Their passion for helping others understand the depth of God's appointed times, shines through every chapter. This book will not only educate but also ignite a deeper desire to walk in God's rhythm of rest, revelation and relationship.

Thank you,

Jennifer Bagnaschi

Jennifer Bagnaschi
Author/Writer/Host/Podcaster
Deep Believer
The Deep Believer Show
E: contact@deepbeliever.com

"For the Father loves the Son, and shows Him all things that He Himself does; and He will show Him greater works than these, **that you may marvel!**" *(John 5:20)*

The Beauty and Biblical Significance of Shabbat

Six months ago, Scott and Amanda Cumbee introduced us to the beauty of Shabbat, a gift from God that we had long overlooked.

For years, we had heard teachings suggesting that it was no longer important, that rest was optional and that Sabbath was merely an Old Testament practice. Yet, when we began to honor Shabbat as God intended, everything changed. It has now become our favorite day of the week, a day where heaven feels near, peace fills our home and our hearts are reset in His presence.

From the very beginning, God Himself modeled rest. "And on the seventh day God ended His work which He had done, and He rested on the seventh day from all His work which He had done. Then God blessed the seventh day and sanctified it" (Genesis 2:2–3). Shabbat was not man's idea; it was God's. He didn't rest because He was weary but because He was finished. He invited us into that same divine rhythm of completion and communion.

When we set aside this holy day, we are declaring that our trust is not in our labor but in our Lord. It's a day to cease striving and to remember that He is our Provider, our Sustainer and our Rest. As the Lord said, "Remember the Sabbath day, to keep it holy" (Exodus 20:8). In Hebrew, the word Shabbat means "to cease" or "to rest," and in that ceasing we find renewal for our souls.

Over these months, Shabbat has brought our family together in ways we couldn't have imagined. We gather around the table, light the candles, pray, worship and invite the Ruach HaKodesh (The Holy Spirit) to dwell richly among us. We can tangibly feel the manifest presence of the Lord during our time of rest in Him. It's as if the busyness of the world fades and all that remains is His peace.

Jesus Himself said, "The Sabbath was made for man, not man for the Sabbath" (Mark 2:27). Shabbat is not a burden, it's a blessing. It's an appointed time where we remember that Jesus is Lord of the Sabbath (Matthew 12:8) and that our ultimate rest is found in Him. As Hebrews 4:9–10 reminds us, "There remains therefore a rest for the people of God. For he who has entered His rest has himself also ceased from his works as God did from His."

Through stillness and worship, the Lord has given us profound revelation; truths we might have missed in the noise of daily life. Shabbat has become a weekly encounter with His presence, a reset for our hearts and a prophetic picture of the eternal rest we will one day enjoy with Him.

We are deeply grateful to Scott and Amanda for reawakening this truth in our hearts. Their obedience to teach the importance of honoring God's rhythm of rest has changed our family forever. What began as a simple act of obedience has become a beautiful tradition of joy, worship and revelation.

Shabbat Shalom: May the peace of God, which surpasses all understanding, continue to guard our hearts and homes as we rest in Him. We love you guys! Thank you so much for allowing us to be a small part of this amazing book!

Justin and Kasey

Justin and Kasey Greenwell
Ministers and Kingdom Entrepreneurs,

Get Your Rhythm Back!

As Scott and Amanda Cumbee reveal in *The Gift of Shabbat*, everything in creation vibrates with its own divine frequency, a rhythm set in motion by the Creator Himself. Yet in our overworked, overstimulated world of deadlines, drive-thru dinners and nonstop notifications, that rhythm has been drowned out. We've forgotten how to breathe, how to rest, how to *be still*.

Shabbat is the answer. It's not just about taking a day off; it's about realigning your soul with the heartbeat of Heaven. It's about restoring the rhythm of family, faith and fellowship. It's about setting aside the noise of life to meet with the King of Kings in sacred rest — the most important "appointment" you'll ever keep.

If you've never experienced the beauty of the Sabbath, *The Gift of Shabbat* is the perfect place to begin. Let Scott and Amanda guide you step-by-step into the joy, peace and laughter that fill this holy day. Don't worry about getting every Hebrew word right; just relax, be present and enjoy time with your Father in Heaven. That's what Shabbat is all about.

So take a breath. Unplug from every screen, step outside, feel the grass beneath your feet and let Friday's setting sun remind you that this is your *prophetic pause*, your invitation to reconnect with the rhythm of creation. Remember: you can't "mess up" a gift. As Yeshua said, "The Sabbath was made for man, not man for the Sabbath" (Mark 2:27). Just accept it. Enjoy it. Let it renew you — and then do it all again next week.

To your (physical and spiritual) health,

Scott Laird, ND
A Rood Awakening! International
The Health Awakening
aroodawakening.tv
LairdWellness.com

Dedication

We dedicate this work first and foremost to our Heavenly Father, **YeHoVaH**, who has graciously allowed us the opportunity to share His truth with His people. All honor and glory belong to Him alone. We give thanks to His Son, **Yeshua**, our Savior, Redeemer and soon-coming King. It is our deepest joy to prepare ourselves as His bride, set apart, consecrated and awaiting His return.

After many years of serving Him, these recent seasons have revealed to us in greater measure just how merciful and gracious He truly is. His love sustains us, His Word directs and His Rauch Kodesh *(Holy Spirit)* strengthens us. To Him we owe everything.

This book is also dedicated to our three beloved children, **Faith, Samuel and Grace**. You have each been a blessing to us in countless ways. Thank you for your prayers, encouragement and your help in bringing this project to life. It is our greatest honor to raise you in the truth, teaching you to love YeHoVaH and to be ready for the coming of our King. We are so blessed by each of you.

With special love and gratitude, we thank **Mama Rose** for the many hours she gave in helping with editing. Amanda and I love you dearly and we all treasure the life you live before your family. Your prayers, guidance and steadfast support have been a light to us.

We also extend heartfelt thanks to **Grandma Betty**, whose prayers and encouragement have lifted us continually during these months of preparation. Sharing Shabbat with you as a family has been a joy and a gift beyond words.

We honor and love you **Pastor Mark Biltz and the family of El Shaddai Ministries**. Pastor, you have been a true blessing to our household walking with us in the Spirit through your faithful teaching of Torah. Your heart for the Father and your dedication to His people have not only reached the nations but have also touched our family. We are grateful for the light you carry and the love you share so generously. Your ministry feels like extended family to us; we rejoice that we get to walk this journey of faith alongside you building the Body of the Messiah.

With heartfelt love and gratitude to **Jennifer Bagnaschi and Deep Believer Ministries** - We love you and your family. We are so thankful for your ministry. Together we rejoice as co-laborers in proclaiming the gospel to the nations. Your faith and dedication inspire us to press forward in the calling we share in Yeshua the Messiah.

With deep appreciation and love for **Justin, Kasey and the Greenwell Family** - We are deeply thankful for your friendship, faith and hearts for the Kingdom. May you continue to pursue the absolute truth, inspire and strengthen others in the Kingdom of Yehovah. Together, we rejoice as co-laborers in proclaiming the gospel of Yeshua to the nations.

Finally, to our family, friends and all who have stood with us in prayer, encouragement and inquiry, thank you. Every question, every conversation and every word of support has helped strengthen this work. May YeHoVaH bless you richly for your faithfulness.

With grateful hearts, *Thank you, We Love You All*.

Scott & Amanda Cumbee

In Loving Memory and Honor of the Faithful

This book is lovingly dedicated to the **patriarchs and matriarchs of the faith**, those who gave their lives and never turned back, even though it cost them everything. Their sacrifice and steadfast devotion has left an eternal impact upon our lives, our children and generations yet to come.

We carry the flame of the Gospel because of those who came before us. They blazed the trail so that we and countless others might hear the truth and walk in the light. Many of their names may never be remembered on this earth but in Heaven their faithfulness echoes. One day, everything they have done will be revealed as glory unto our Father, the King of the Universe and to His Son, Yeshua the Messiah.

To our loved ones who have gone on before us, we remember you with gratitude. We honor every faithful servant's courage who stood firm in the face of trials, persecution and even death. Because of you, we now have the opportunity to know the truth and to share it with a lost and dying generation.

We pledge to take up the mantle, to proclaim the Word and to prepare the way for the coming of our King. Thank you for your faith, example and unwavering love for YeHoVaH.

A Personal Tribute

I also want to take a moment to honor my father, **Eddie Leon Cumbee**. Daddy, thank you for everything you've done for me and our family. I honor you and I love you deeply. You taught me how to forgive much, forgive often and to love always. The difference you have made in the lives of so many people is immeasurable. Your strength, example and heart for others continue to inspire me.

A Call to Prepare Your Heart

Warning, once you begin reading this book, you will be faced with the absolute truth that has the power to change your life for eternity. The revelation of Shabbat is not simply information; it is an invitation from our Father Himself to step into His covenant rest, His blessing and His eternal promises.

We want to thank you for the opportunity to share the treasure we have found in Him, a revelation that has forever transformed our lives. Now, it is being placed into your hands as a gift.

Before you continue, we ask you to pause and consider, will you humble yourself, set aside distractions and past teachings and open your heart to the Father? Will you allow His Ruach Kodesh (*Set Apart Spirit, Holy Spirit*) to guide you into truth as you read?

If your answer is yes, then we invite you to pray the following prayer with all sincerity, preparing your heart for the encounter you are about to have with the Spirit of Shabbat.

Prayer

Father, I thank You for the opportunity to open this book and seek Your absolute truth. I come before You, asking Ruach HaKodesh (*Set Apart Spirit, The Holy Spirit*), to reveal to me if what I am about to read is relevant for today, has not passed away but is eternal truth that flows from Your heart. You never change and Your Word endures forever.

Heavenly Father, I come before You with a humble and sincere heart, desiring to know You more deeply and to walk in the fullness of Your truth. I lay down every preconceived idea, tradition and distraction that may hinder me from receiving what You want to reveal. Cleanse my heart and renew my mind so that I may discern Your voice clearly and embrace the covenant You are inviting me into. I lay aside every preconceived thought and every past teaching that does not align with You. I open my heart and mind before You in humility.

Thank You for giving us Your sacred Shabbat as a gift and a sign of Your eternal covenant. On this set apart day of rest, prepare me to receive the knowledge and revelation You want to impart through these pages. Give me an open heart to embrace Your absolute truth and a clear mind to discern Your ways.

Open my eyes to see Your Shabbat not as a burden but as a blessing that leads me into Your eternal rest. Teach me that if I genuinely love You, I will keep Your commandments with joy and gladness. Let the words within this book prepare me to enter Your covenant rest and may they plant seeds of eternal truth that will change my life forever if I walk in obedience.

Father, I ask You to reveal the fullness of Your Shabbat, that in honoring it I may testify that You never change, Your Word is living; Your promises are everlasting. May this book bring me more than knowledge. Allow it to be a doorway into Your presence leading me to walk in the freedom, renewal and eternal covenant. In the mighty name of Yeshua (*Jesus*), the Messiah, Amen.

Unless you understand the heart behind our writing, some things may sound unfamiliar or even uncomfortable at first. What you are about to read is not just a collection of teachings; it is a journey into truths that have been hidden, words that have been altered and rhythms that have been interrupted. Once this is made clear, everything else will start to make sense. The world tried to bury them, religion tried to rename them, the enemy tried to erase them but they were never destroyed. For generations there have been treasures of covenant that were not lost but deliberately preserved by our Father in Heaven. This book is part of that unveiling. As you read, you will notice I use the name YeHoVaH instead of simply saying "GOD" or "LORD." This is intentional. The original Hebrew Scriptures have the four letters יהוה (*YHVH, Tetragrammaton*) over 6,827 times, yet many Bible translations replaced them with titles like *"Adonai,* LORD, Yahweh, Jehovah, or *HaShem (The Name).*" But YeHoVaH said, "This is My Name forever, and this is My memorial unto all generations" (***Exodus 3:15***). His name matters. It reveals who He is in covenant. His Son's name Yeshua, not the later English form "Jesus" literally means "YeHoVaH Saves." Every time we speak the name *Yeshua*, we are declaring the salvation of *YeHoVaH*. This is not a matter of legalism or language pride; it is about restoring what has been removed, covered and banned to be spoken.

Shabbat, the seventh day Sabbath is YeHoVaH's divine rhythm. From the beginning, He blessed and sanctified the seventh day (***Genesis 2:2-3***). Yet this too was replaced, forgotten or changed by man. But just like His name, Shabbat was never abolished. It was buried under tradition and now YeHoVaH is restoring it to His people. When I speak of the "rhythm of Shabbat," I am not talking about a rule. I am talking about a holy pattern of time set up at creation. Six days we work. On the seventh day we rest, not just physically but spiritually. We reconnect with the Father and reset our hearts. We remember who we are in Him. Shabbat is the heartbeat of heaven that brings rhythm, restoration and relationship.

So please hear this! What you are about to read may challenge what you have been taught but it will awaken what has been hidden inside your spirit. At just eight years old, I made the greatest decision of my life. With all my heart, I surrendered to Yeshua (*Jesus*) the Messiah. I asked Him to forgive my sins and confessed with my mouth that He died for me and rose again. From that moment, I promised to live for Him all my days. Soon after, YeHoVaH gave me a dream that would mark my destiny. I saw a man clothed like one from biblical times, walking toward a massive, ancient, closed door. On the right side etched into the cornerstone of the door was an engraving shining like gold, radiant with glory. At that time, I did not understand. Years later the revelation came when I was forty-four years of age. The engraving was His true name. Today, you hold a key to unlock the treasure chest of His covenant. Once opened, you will begin to see with new eyes, hear with new ears and walk in deeper purpose and power because of the covenant name of our Father: יְהֹוָה (YeHoVaH).

"*It is the glory of God to conceal a thing: but the honour of kings is to search out a matter*" (**Proverbs 25:2** KJV).

This book is not just a message. It is a map to the treasure.

Let us begin the journey.

INTRODUCTION

"The fear of [YeHoVaH] the LORD is the beginning of wisdom" (**Proverbs 9:10** KJV).

The Scriptures declare this with clarity, yet for many it drifts past like the passing of wind across a quiet pond. You see its ripples for a moment and then they vanish as though they were never there. Too often we treat the fear of God that way, acknowledging it briefly but never letting it reach the depths of our hearts. Yet this fear is not a relic of the Old Covenant [*Tanakh*] nor is it an empty phrase for us to admire. It is the very posture that holds eternity in place, that steadies the heart in a world of deception and prepares every soul for the day we must stand before the Judge of all.

Solomon, the man to whom God gave unmatched wisdom and wealth, surveyed the whole span of earthly pleasures. He built palaces, planted vineyards, gathered riches beyond counting and tasted every desire of man. Yet his conclusion was not to chase after these things, for he recognized they are no more than grasping at the wind.

I remember asking a man to read one Sunday night at the church I pastored. He shared how he was washing out his hog houses earlier that day. In that moment, I thought about the prodigal son who had wasted everything, came to himself in the mire and realized that in his father's house there was always provision. In the same way, the man reading that night confessed that his spiritual eyes were opened. He realized what true wealth was. He recognized that it was all emptiness without God. He said plainly: *"I was chasing after the wind."*

When he spoke those words, it was as though heaven carved them into my heart. I can still hear his voice today. It shook me because it was not just his testimony; it was Solomon's cry all over again: *all is vanity, chasing after the wind.* I realized, if King Solomon who once had what others dreamed of, could stand broken and confess the futility of it all, then the only true riches are found in fearing God and keeping His commandments. His confession became a warning to me and a reminder that the Father's house is the only place of provision. Leaving it is to starve; returning is to live. All else fades and proves empty.

Only obedience, rooted in holy reverence will remain. Among those commandments is the call to remember the Sabbath, a command so vital that YeHoVaH Himself placed it in the heart of His covenant. He did not set it up to burden us but to draw us near to Him in fellowship. Every seven days He calls His children aside, not for a ritual but for a relationship. The Sabbath is His appointed time, a weekly covenant meeting where He reveals Himself to His Bride. Yet, men have exchanged this gift for traditions and excuses, convincing themselves that His Word has changed. Please do not let your hearts be deceived through the traditions of men or our church forefathers. The Judge will not weigh our lives by the customs of men but by the Word of God. Neglecting His Sabbath is to ignore His voice. Honoring the Sabbath is to embrace His covenant love.

The fear of YeHoVaH is not terror that drives us away; it is holy reverence that brings us close enough to hate sin and cling to His ways. When Joseph stood against temptation in Egypt, his words were simple: *"How then can I do this great wickedness, and sin against God?"* He was not afraid of discovery; he was ruled by reverence. That same spirit of reverence is still very much needed today. For without the fear of God, worship becomes shallow, preaching becomes entertainment and the church becomes indistinguishable from the world.

Eternity is never far. One breath divides us from judgment, one heartbeat from forever. Paul understood this when he wrote that all must appear before the judgment seat of Messiah, to give account of every deed. Knowing the terror of YeHoVaH, He persuaded men with urgency. Eternity was no theory for Him; it was certainty. It must be so for us as well.

The fear of God is not bondage, nor is it the spirit of fear that Scripture says leads to torment. The spirit He gives is power, love and a sound mind. His fear, however, is clean, enduring and forever. When it grips the soul, it breaks chains and opens our eyes. Those who tremble before God no longer tremble before men. Those who honor His Word cannot be deceived by human-caused traditions. Messiah Himself warned: *"Fear not them which kill the body but rather fear Him who is able to destroy both soul and body in hell"* (**Matthew 10:28**). The fear of man enslaves but the fear of God frees.

Even Yeshua, the Son of God, walked in this reverence. Isaiah declared that the Spirit of YeHoVaH would rest upon Him and that He would delight in the fear of YeHoVaH. If the sinless Son of God needed this posture, how much more do we, frail and flawed require it?

And what does this reverence produce? Life! *"The fear of [YeHoVaH] the LORD is a fountain of life, to depart from the snares of death"* (**Proverbs 14:27** KJV). It is the wellspring that keeps us from compromise and draws us deeper into His covenant. The Sabbath itself is a fountain, a weekly renewal where the Father restores our souls and reminds us of who we are. It is no small matter to push aside and refuse His gift.

However, honoring it is to walk in His life. *"... I am come that they might have life, and that they might have it more abundantly"* (**John 10:10** KJV).

The prophets declared that God looks to the one who trembles at His Word. That trembling is not weakness but holy strength. It is the posture of the Bride adorned for her Bridegroom, refusing the counterfeit ways of this world. Every Sabbath kept in reverence is a declaration: *"I am Yours. I will not be separated from You in this life, and I will not be separated from You in eternity."*

Never forget this truth: we need God, but He desires a relationship with us. The question is not whether He wants His people, He has already proven that through the shed blood of His Son. The question is whether we truly desire Him.

- Do we want Him enough to forsake the fleeting winds of pleasure?
- Do we want Him enough to obey what He has spoken, even when men tell us otherwise?
- Do we want Him enough to remember His Sabbath, to cherish His covenant and to live in holy reverence until we see Him face to face?

One day every soul will stand before the Almighty, the King of the Universe, a Holy God and in that moment our wisdom, our strength and even our righteousness will be exposed as filthy rags (***Isaiah 64:6***). Only the blood of Yeshua will be able to cover us. Those who live in holy reverence, who fear God, keep His commandments and remember His Sabbath will hear the voice of the Bridegroom calling them into eternal rest.

So let us walk now as His Bride, adorned not with fleeting treasures but with faithfulness, clothed in holy reverence and waiting each week at His appointed time. For the day is coming when the Sabbath will no longer be a rehearsal but an eternal reality and those who love His appearing will enter His rest forever. So let the words of the wisest man seal it with the weight of eternity: *"...Fear [YeHoVaH] God, and keep His commandments: for this is the whole duty of man"* (*Ecclesiastes 12:13* KJV).

Reader Review: *A Life Changing Revelation - A Book Everyone Should Read!* "***The Gift of Shabbat*** *isn't just a book; it's a revelation. Scott and Amanda Cumbee have written something that awakens the heart and renews the soul. As I began reading this book, I felt as if a veil had been lifted. For years, I read Scripture but never truly understood the beauty and depth of the Sabbath. This book opened my eyes to Yehovah's divine rhythm of rest, relationship and renewal. As a nurse, I understand how following protocols can save lives. In the same way, when I follow my Father's commands, everything changes. This truth came alive as I read, showing that the Sabbath is not a burden but a blessing, a sacred invitation to walk in peace and restoration. Each chapter is filled with wisdom, scripture and life-changing insight. The way Scott and Amanda teach about the Torah and the true Sabbath is both powerful and personal. It reached deep into my spirit. I didn't just read this book; I experienced it. I found myself slowing down, listening for Yehovah's voice and seeing His plan with new clarity. Every page drew me closer to Yeshua. If you've ever wondered what the Sabbath really means or if you have longed for a deeper walk with Yehovah, this book will change your life. It's not just information; it's transformation. This is a must-read for every believer who desires truth, rest and intimacy with Yehovah."*
By: Rose, Nurse and Sabbath Keeper

Chapter 1
The Verdict of Eternity: Torah and Shabbat Still Stand

From the time I was young, I was fascinated by the courtroom. I enjoyed watching lawyers skillfully take facts, ask questions and paint pictures so clearly that no jury could deny the truth. For a season, I thought I would become a lawyer and present the absolute truth in the courts of men. One day as I was driving my truck to college, Ruach HaKodesh (*Set Apart Spirit, The Holy Spirit*) spoke to me: *"I did not call you to argue the laws of men. I called you to proclaim My Word. There are people who need to hear what I have given you to say."*

That day I realized my true calling, not to stand before earthly judges but to present the unshakable case of YeHoVaH's Word. It was not to argue man's law but to declare God's truth. Now, dear reader, will you accept the responsibilities of becoming a juror and not a bystander? If so, you have solemnly affirmed your duty as the juror of this chapter. This is not merely a story; it is your courtroom. Here, the evidence will be presented before you. You will hear the testimony, examine the facts and weigh the arguments.

You are not allowed to remain neutral or detached. As a juror, you must lean in, listen carefully and at the end of this chapter you will be asked to give your verdict. The responsibility rests upon you to discern truth from falsehood and light from darkness. Every paragraph is an exhibit. Every passage is a witness starting with Exhibit A through Exhibit Z. Every word is placed before you for consideration. This is your trial, your chapter and your verdict; you must decide. Let us begin.

Has the Torah, the commandments of YeHoVaH, been abolished, or do they still stand, revealed and fulfilled in Yeshua, the Living Word made flesh?

Exhibit A: The Word Became Flesh

John 1:1-2, 14 declares: "In the beginning was the Word, and the Word was with God, and the Word was God… And the Word was made flesh and dwelt among us."

That Word was not an invention. It was the Torah, the revealed instructions of YeHoVaH. Yeshua did not come to erase it; He came to embody it. If Yeshua is the Torah in flesh, how could He abolish Himself? He could not; it would be impossible.

Exhibit B: Yeshua's Own Testimony

Matthew 5:17-19 records His sworn words: "Don't think that I have come to abolish the Torah or the Prophets. I have come not to abolish but to complete…"

Until heaven and earth pass away, not so much as a *yud [jot, also part of the Father's four-letter Hebrew name, YHVH]* or a stroke will pass from the Torah. Heaven and earth still stand. Therefore, so does the Torah.

Exhibit C: The New Covenant Promise

Jeremiah 31:31-33 makes it plain: "I will put my [*Torah*] law in their inward parts, and write it in their hearts…"

The New Covenant does not replace Torah; it relocates it, no longer on tablets of stone but written into human hearts by the Spirit of YeHoVaH.

Exhibit D: Paul's Defense of the Law

Romans 3:31 questions: "Do we then make void the [*Torah*] law through faith? God forbid yea, we establish the law."

Romans 7:12: "Wherefore the [*Torah*] law is holy, and the commandment holy, and just, and good."

Faith in Yeshua does not cancel the Torah; it proves it. Paul did not preach lawlessness; he preached grace that empowers obedience.

Exhibit E: Love Defined by Obedience

John 14:15: "If ye love me, keep my commandments."

Love is not free from Torah; it is faithfulness to it.

1 John 5:3 echoes: "For this is the love of God, that we keep his commandments: and his commandments are not grievous."

Love for YeHoVaH is proven in obedience, not in casting off His commandments.

Exhibit F: Torah in the Kingdom to Come

Isaiah 2:2-3 prophesies: "For out of Zion shall go forth the [*Torah*] law, and the word of the Lord from Jerusalem."

Even in the Messianic Kingdom, Torah goes forth.

Revelation 12:17 identifies the faithful as those who "keep the commandments of God *and* the testimony of [*Yeshua*]Jesus Christ." Both are essential.

Exhibit G: The Apostles' Testimony

James 1:22: "Be ye doers of the word, and not hearers only, deceiving your own selves."

Acts 24:14: "I believe all things which are written in the [*Torah*] law and in the prophets."

The apostles never abandoned the Torah. They upheld it in the Spirit of Yeshua.

Exhibit H: The Sabbath Commandment

Exodus 20:8-11: "Remember the sabbath day, to keep it holy… the seventh day is the sabbath of [*YeHoVaH*] the Lord thy God."

It is written in stone, commanded forever. Of all instructions, YeHoVaH begins this one with "Remember" because He knew men would try to forget it.

Exhibit I: Yeshua's Custom Was Shabbat

Luke 4:16: "As his custom was, he went into the synagogue on the sabbath day, and stood up for to read."

Yeshua kept Shabbat, not Sunday or a day chosen by man. Shabbat was sanctified in Genesis.

Exhibit J: The Apostles Kept Shabbat

Acts 17:2: "Paul, as his manner was, went in unto them, and three sabbath days reasoned with them…"

Acts 18:4: "He reasoned in the synagogue every sabbath, and persuaded the Jews and the Greeks."

The apostles upheld Shabbat decades after Yeshua's resurrection. Why were they not informed if the day had profoundly changed?

Exhibit K: The Change to Sunday

History records the truth. In the 4th century, Emperor Constantine decreed:

"On the venerable day of the Sun let the magistrates and people… rest."

This was not YeHoVaH's will. It was Rome's compromise with pagan sun worship. Later, church councils claimed authority to move the Sabbath to Sunday. But nowhere does YeHoVaH change His command.

Exhibit L: Yeshua's Warning Against Traditions

Mark 7:9: "Full well ye reject the commandment of God, that ye may keep your own tradition."

Changing Shabbat to Sunday is the clearest fulfillment of this warning. Tradition has tried to override God's command. His Word is still eternal.

Exhibit M: The Sabbath Remains for Believers

Hebrews 4:9: "There remaineth therefore a rest [*sabbatismos, Greek meaning of Sabbath*] to the people of God."

The word literally means "a Sabbath-keeping." Shabbat is not abolished in the New Covenant, it remains.

Exhibit N: Shabbat at Creation

Genesis 2:2-3: "And on the seventh day God ended his work which he had made; and he rested on the seventh day... And God blessed the seventh day, and sanctified it."

Ladies and gentlemen of the jury, before there was Israel, before there was Moses, before there was Sinai, there was Shabbat. It was sanctified in creation itself. Can man undo what the Creator set apart before sin ever entered the world? It is impossible.

Exhibit O: The Sabbath as Covenant Sign

Exodus 31:16-17: "Wherefore the children of Israel shall keep the sabbath... for a perpetual covenant. It is a sign between me and the children of Israel for ever."

The Sabbath is YeHoVaH's sign of covenant forever. If it was abolished, then so was His covenant. But His covenant stands and so does the Sabbath.

Exhibit P: The Prophets Confirm the Sabbath

Isaiah 56:6-7: "Also the sons of the stranger, that join themselves to [YeHoVaH] the Lord... Every one that keepeth the sabbath from polluting it, and taketh hold of my covenant; Even them will I bring to my holy mountain."

Isaiah 66:23: "From one sabbath to another, shall all flesh come to worship before me, saith [*YeHoVaH*] the Lord."

The prophets saw the Sabbath not abolished but magnified, even for the nations.

Exhibit Q: Yeshua is Lord of the Sabbath

Matthew 12:8: "For the Son of man is Lord even of the sabbath day."

If Yeshua is LORD of the Sabbath, then the Sabbath belongs to Him. How can He abolish what He rules over? Instead, He clarified how it should be kept by preserving the Father's command.

Exhibit R: Early Church Fathers Testify

Even after the apostles, many early believers kept Sabbath.

- In 90 AD, early writing documents like the *Didache* [*Teaching of the Twelve Apostles*] show that believers were gathering often, sometimes even on the first day but the seventh-day Sabbath remained central.
- In 135 AD, Persecution after the Bar Kokhba Revolt the Jewish identity became dangerous in the Roman Empire. Many Gentile Christians distanced themselves from Sabbath-keeping to avoid persecution.
- In 150 -200 AD, early church fathers like Justin Martyr began promoting Sunday worship to honor the

resurrection. This was tradition, not a biblical command.

The historical record shows Shabbat remained alive in the body until persecution forced compromise.

Exhibit S: The Cost of Lawlessness

Matthew 7:23: "And then will I profess unto them, I never knew you: depart from me, ye that work iniquity."

"Iniquity" is the Greek word *anomia* lawlessness, Torah-lessness. Yeshua warns that those who cast off His Father's commandments will be rejected, even if they claim His name.

Exhibit T: Torah as the Standard of Judgment

Revelation 20:12: "And the dead were judged out of those things which were written in the books, according to their works."

The Judge of the Universe will not measure us by traditions of men. He will use His own Word, the Torah (*law*) as the standard.

Exhibit U: The Unchanging Nature of God

Malachi 3:6: "For I am [*YeHoVaH*] the Lord, I change not."

Hebrews 13:8: "[*Yeshua*], Jesus Christ the same yesterday, and today, and for ever."

If YeHoVaH and Yeshua are unchanging, then their commandments are unchanging. To claim Torah has been abolished is to claim God has changed. But He declares: *"I change not."*

Exhibit V: Victory Through Obedience

Deuteronomy 28 outlines blessings for obedience, prosperity, fruitfulness and victory over enemies. Obedience to Torah is not bondage; it is the pathway to victory. Disobedience brings curses, not blessings. The choice is yours.

Exhibit W: Warnings Against Lawlessness

2 Thessalonians 2:7-12 warns of the "mystery of iniquity" (*anomia - Torah-lessness)* that will deceive many in the last days. The enemy's plan is to turn hearts away from Torah but YeHoVaH's remnant resists the lie.

Exhibit X: The Crucifixion Confirms the Law

Romans 3:31: "Do we then make void the law through faith? God forbid: yea, we establish the law."

The crucifixion did not erase Torah, it confirmed it. Yeshua's death paid the penalty for our law breaking but it did not erase the law itself. A pardon cancels the punishment, not the law.

Exhibit Y: Yeshua Rested in the Grave on Shabbat

Luke 23:56: "And they returned, and prepared spices and ointments; and rested the sabbath day according to the commandment."

Even in His death, Yeshua honored Sabbath. He rested in the tomb on the seventh day, then rose on the first day. His life and death both confirm the Sabbath.

Exhibit Z: Zion's Eternal Sabbath

Isaiah 66:22-23: "For as the new heavens and the new earth… it shall come to pass, that from one sabbath to another, shall all flesh come to worship before me, saith the Lord."

From creation to new creation, Sabbath stands. In Zion's future, all flesh will gather to worship on the Sabbath. If it remains in the new heavens and new earth, how can it be abolished today?

The Juror's Verdict

You have now heard Exhibits A through Z. The case has been fully presented. Every angle has been covered. The evidence is clear:

- Yeshua is the Living Word, the Torah in flesh.
- He declared the Torah would not be abolished.
- The New Covenant writes it on our hearts.
- The apostles upheld it.
- The prophets confirmed it.
- The Sabbath still stands.
- History reveals men changed it, not GOD.
- From Genesis to Revelation, Torah and Sabbath still remain.

As a juror, you must now deliver your verdict for this chapter: **Has the Sabbath been abolished or does it stand?**

The evidence allows no reasonable doubt. The Sabbath and Torah still stand. It remains with you and I today and for eternity. Yeshua reigns as LORD of the Sabbath and embodiment of Torah.

The Trial Beyond This Chapter

Now that you have delivered your verdict, the trial shifts. The case has been proven; the Sabbath and Torah still stand. Your task is no longer to weigh evidence; it is to learn the rhythm of life that flows from it.

The rhythm is Shabbat. To live for Yeshua, the Living Torah, is not only to labor in His name but to rest in Him as He commanded. True obedience is not endless sacrifice; it is resting where the Father said to rest, walking where He said to walk and living by every word that goes forth from His mouth. One day, each of us will stand before the Judge of the Universe. The question will not be, *"Were you working for Me?"* but rather, *"Did you truly know Me and honor My Father's commandments?"*

You may have been taught to work, sacrifice and serve but the Father says, *"Obedience is better than sacrifice."* Many will discover too late that they were laboring in their own strength while ignoring His rest. **Ephesians 2:2** Paul explains *"...according to the prince of the power of the air, the spirit that now worketh in the children of disobedience."*

The truth never changes. The remaining chapters of this book will not call you into heavier burdens; they will teach you the way of obedience, the way of rest in Yeshua, the Living Torah. They will show you how to live in harmony with the Father's will. Only by walking with Him and resting in Him will you be prepared for the day you stand before Him.

Chapter 2
The Unbroken Covenant: Shabbat and His Commandments Still Stand

When the Hebrew Scriptures were translated into Greek, subtle changes in wording began to shift how people understood YeHoVaH's covenant. The word *berith* (*covenant*) was often translated into testament and *mitzvot* (*commandments*) simply became *law*. Over time, this gave the impression that what YeHoVaH had spoken was outdated, heavy and destined to pass away. However, the covenant of YeHoVaH has never been revoked. His commandments were never meant to be viewed as burdens but as life-giving instructions for His people.

The Father sent His only begotten Son, Yeshua, not to abolish these things but to bring them to fullness and fulfill them. He said plainly, *"Do not think-I came that I might breach (break) the Torah- or the prophets. I came not that I might fulfill (complete or end) but rather that I might fill (the Torah) to overflowing, abundantly*overflowing! Truly, I say unto you, until heaven and earth pass away- not one yod from Torah, nor even the tip of a yod, will pass away-until all of these words are carried out"* (**Matthew 5:17–18** HTV). Heaven and earth remain and so do His commandments. Fulfillment does not mean cancellation, it means bringing forth the heart and purpose of what was already spoken.

The Torah as a Mirror of Sin

Paul explains that the Torah is what reveals sin, *"for by the [Torah] law is the knowledge of sin"* (**Romans 3:20** KJV). Without the commandments, there would be no measure of righteousness or rebellion. Sabbath, like the rest of YeHoVaH's instructions, was given to show us His righteousness and our continual need for His grace. It is not bondage but freedom because it keeps us from walking in ignorance and shows us what pleases our Father.

Yeshua taught the commandments in love. He never lessened them but revealed their depth; to lust is adultery in the heart and to hate is murder in seed form (***Matthew 5:21-28*** KJV). He showed us that obedience is rooted in love, not legalism. This is why He declared: **"If ye love me, keep my commandments"** (***John 14:15*** KJV). Our love for Him is proven in our willingness to honor what He has spoken from the beginning.

Sabbath: The Sign of the Covenant

From the very creation of the world, the Sabbath was set apart. *"And on the seventh day, God ended His work which He had made, and He rested on the seventh day from all His work which He had made. And God blessed the seventh day, and sanctified it; because that in it He had rested from all his work which God created and made"* (***Genesis 2:2-3*** MBB). Long before Israel, Sinai or even the Jews and Gentiles, the Sabbath was holy. This day was a personal invitation to come and build a relationship with the Father. It was blessed and sanctified as YeHoVaH's own day of rest.

Later, when the Hebrews left Egypt, He confirmed it as an everlasting sign and put specific instructions in place, *"Wherefore the children of Israel shall keep the sabbath, to observe the sabbath throughout their generations, for a perpetual covenant. It is a sign between me and the children of Israel for ever: for in six days [YeHoVaH] the LORD made heaven and earth, and on the seventh day he* rested, and was refreshed." (**Exodus 31:16-17** KJV). A "perpetual covenant" cannot expire because Yehovah does not change. His Word reminds us, *"[Yeshua the Messiah] Jesus Christ the same yesterday, and to day, and for ever"* (**Hebrews 13:8** KJV). If He has not changed, then neither has His covenant.

The prophet Isaiah pointed to the Sabbath as a key to delight in YeHoVaH's presence, *"If thou turn away thy foot from the sabbath, from doing thy pleasure (jobs, work, or businesses) on my holy day; and call the sabbath a delight, the holy of [YeHoVaH] the LORD, honourable; and shalt honour him, not doing thine own ways, nor finding thine own pleasure, nor speaking thine own words: then shalt thou delight thyself in [YeHoVaH] the LORD; and I will cause thee to ride upon the high places of the earth (make you successful), and feed thee with the heritage of Jacob thy father: for the mouth of [YeHoVaH] the LORD hath spoken it"* (**Isaiah 58:13-14** KJV). Sabbath is not just a day of rest; it is a day of delight, a day to encounter YeHoVaH's presence, to cease striving and remember that He is our source.

Endurance of the Saints

Even at the close of the age, the Sabbath and the commandments are still present. Revelation declares: *"Here is the patience of the saints, here are they that keep the commandments of God, and the faith of [Yeshua] Jesus"* (**Revelation 14:12** KJV). The final generation is marked by this union, obedience to YeHoVaH's commandments and faith in Yeshua. The two cannot be separated. Faith without obedience is dead and obedience without faith is powerless. Together they reveal the endurance of the true saints.

Chapter 3
The Origin and Covenant of the Sabbath: A Gift from the Beginning

Sabbath is often spoken of as Shabbat, which is the seventh day of the week. These two words are used interchangeably. It is not just a day of rest but a time to honor and celebrate a divine appointment that was orchestrated from the beginning of time by YeHoVaH for all humanity. It is considered one of the very first things in the Scriptures that YeHoVaH sanctified. Why would He do this or what was His purpose for this day to be separate from all other days? The seventh day stands for something deep in the heart of the Father, a pattern of rest, a space for a relationship and a prophetic picture of the future Messiah, Yeshua. This is a day set in stone that is not up for discussion on what time it occurs. ***Genesis 2:2*** is an extremely specific verse. It is a time that we set ourselves apart each week from sunset on Friday to sunset on Saturday. This is the true Sabbath day.

The Origin of the Shabbat

Shabbat began in the garden. On the seventh day, Elohim "rested;" in Hebrew "*shavat*" which means to cease, stop, rest or sit down. It is an act of obedience to rest from our productive six days of work to meet with our creator. Just as Elohim stopped creating, we need to stop our productivity and the cares of this world at the entrance door to Shabbat. This is an appointment, invitation, a set apart day for You and me to separate from the holy and profane. It is a time to lay down our tools, pleasures and plans as we trust that Elohim will provide what we release. It is an act of obedience trusting that YeHoVaH is our provider [*YeHoVaH Yireh*], not our own efforts or righteousness (**Leviticus 23: 1-3**).

What Makes the Sabbath Special

The Sabbath is a special time that the Father ordained to enjoy and dwell with His creation. Did you know the word Shabbat in Hebrew is related to "shevet" which means to abide and dwell (**Genesis 3:8-9**)? The same way YeHoVaH desired to have a relationship with Adam and Eve is the same way He wants a relationship with you. YeHoVaH comes to abide and dwell on the Sabbath, a sanctified set apart time to fellowship with His creation. This is the Bride's opportunity to honor her Bridegroom, Yeshua, before the world and learn His Torah **John 1:1**. *"Whosoever, therefore shall confess me before men, him will I confess also before my Father which is in heaven. But whosoever shall deny me before men, him will I also deny before my Father which is in heaven"* (**Matthew 10:32-33** MBB). YeHoVaH created Adam the absolute best bride but she did not have any works. She was not proven to be faithful, neither was Adam. However, the last Adam, "Yeshua," Yehovah's only begotten Son was tried, crucified, resurrected and became our Redeemer. The Bride that He will be given must be tested and refined before the world, proving her worthiness for the glorious Marriage of the Lamb, Yeshua. Queen Esther prepared herself for the king. You and I must also prepare ourselves for our King. This is what the *Book of Remembrance* in **Malachi 3:6** is all about. How do we come in covenant together with YeHoVaH? We are to honor His commandments and keep His appointed feast days (*modiem*). These are vital preparations that are necessary for us to enter into covenant with YeHoVaH. The consecrated acts are not only symbolic but a prophetic shadow of the kingdom to come, *"There remaineth therefore a rest to the people of God"* (**Hebrews 4:9** KJV). So, I pray that if you are not already in relationship with YeHoVaH, that you will begin this covenant journey today and keep the weekly Shabbat appointment. The purpose of every seventh day is for the Bride to rest, remember and dwell in the presence of her Groom, "Yeshua."

A Sign and a Covenant for Eternity: Exodus 31:13

Just like a wedding ring is a reminder that you are set apart for your spouse, Shabbat is a sign of the covenant between YeHoVaH and the Bride. Observing Shabbat weekly reveals our identity as "The Bride" of Yeshua the Messiah. It is a pure relationship that is *Kodesh* (*set-apart, holy*) unto the Father, YeHoVaH for His glory and purpose. Do you believe God is the "… same yesterday, today, and forever more" (***Hebrews 13:8*** KJV)? If so, then He has not changed but man has and passed the traditions down from generation to generation. Through man's disobedience to God, man lost his true treasure. My friend, there is still hope of restoration with the Father, YeHoVaH, and that is through His Son, Yeshua. As believers of Yeshua, He is our eternal Sabbath rest (***Hebrews 4:9-10***). Every Sabbath is an opportunity to honor our Father's Word or to deny Him. *"…And, as his custom was, he went into the synagogue on the sabbath day, and stood up for to read"* (***Luke 4:16*** KJV). This proves that Yeshua also kept the Sabbath by honoring His Father. What we sow today we will reap later. Take the time for Him now; He will take the time for you eternally.

Should We Honor the Sabbath Today

Yes, most definitely. You and I have the opportunity to host the King of the Universe. Sabbath is a permanent regulation whether we decide to attend it or not. You may have thought His set apart day is just for the Jews, but you have been misled. According to ***Isaiah 56:6-7*** KJV *"Also the sons of the* *stranger, that join themselves to [YeHoVaH] the LORD, to serve him, and to love the name of [YeHoVaH] the LORD, to be his servants, every one that keepth the sabbath from polluting it, and taketh hold of my covenant; Even them will I bring to my holy mountain, and make them joyful in my house of prayer..."* we will be blessed. The Sabbath is a gift to us to celebrate Shabbat with the Father, Yeshua and Ruach HaKodesh (*Set Apart Spirit, The Holy Spirit*). It is not a law bondage but a covenant of joy available to all who will enter His rest. The benefits of walking in the fullness of the covenant through Shabbat includes: a greater intimacy with YeHoVaH, your identity as the Bride of Yeshua, prayer and worship, the Father's covering **Psalms 91**, knowing your position in the Kingdom to come, resting from the chaos of the world and treasured time with your family and friends.

Reflection Questions:

1. How might your perspective on rest change if you began to recognize it as a divine time set apart for renewal?
2. Do you feel you have been striving in your own strength lately? How might keeping the Sabbath help reset that?

Declaration

Father, You are my Creator. You have called me to work six days and rest with You on the Sabbath. I surrender my will to You, YeHoVaH, choosing to honor and obey Your commandments. Today, I freely receive the gift of Shabbat and rest in Your finished work from the beginning of time. Amen

Chapter 4
The Spiritual Covenant of Shabbat: A Prophetic Foretaste of Eternity

"Moreover, I gave them my Sabbaths, as a sign between me and them, that they might know that I am [YeHoVaH] the LORD who sanctifies [set apart] them" (**Ezekiel 20:12** ESV). Not only is Shabbat a day of rest but it is also a spiritual appointment, an encounter with the King of the Universe. This is how His Bride openly proves to the world who she genuinely loves. The seventh day was never meant to be just an empty day of laying around and doing absolutely nothing. It is a time to awaken, refresh our minds and align ourselves with the will of the Father, YeHoVaH. Each week we set the table and light the menorah reminding us of who we are and to whom we belong. It is an opportunity to honor the Father's Word [*Yeshua*], that has been set up since the beginning. A time to be forgiven, delivered and revelation being poured out as you study the Scripture. The Scriptures truly come alive in a new and meaningful way that allow you to understand the parallels of what happened then will happen again. The Word is like a mystery but when you are on Father's timetable and honoring Him, the Word unlocks in a powerful way. This allows your inner spirit to be fed and an opportunity to share with others the good news.

A Weekly Covenant with Yehovah

[13] *"Tell the people of Israel, 'You are to observe my Shabbats; for this is a sign between me and you through all your generations; so that you will know that I am [YeHoVaH] Adonai, who sets you apart for me.* [14] *Therefore you are to keep my Shabbat, because it is set apart for you.*

Everyone who treats it as ordinary must be put to death; for whoever does any work on it is to be cut off from his people. On six days work will get done; but the seventh day is Shabbat, for complete rest, set apart for [YeHoVaH] Adonai. Whoever does any work on the day of Shabbat must be put to death. ⁱ⁶ The people of Israel are to keep the Shabbat, to observe Shabbat through all their generations as a perpetual covenant. ¹⁷ It is a sign between me and the people of Israel forever; for in six days [YeHoVaH] Adonai made heaven and earth, but on the seventh day he stopped working and rested" (***Exodus 31:13-17*** CJB). YeHoVaH called Shabbat a sign of His covenant, meaning a mark or a distinguishing feature. Just like a wedding ring is a visible sign of marital covenant between a man and a woman, Shabbat is a visible and lived-out weekly sign of our relationship with the Father, YeHoVaH. Each week as we enter Shabbat, we acknowledge that YeHoVaH is the one who sets us apart. This is not achieved by our own self-righteousness. When we are disconnected from the Father's Word, the absolute truth, we are merely serving our own idols through our own efforts, seeking stability in what cannot satisfy. In doing so, we will never reach His *Kodesh* (*Spirit of Apartness, Holiness*). The Word states, *"... all our righteousnesses are as filthy rags..."* (***Isaiah 64:6*** KJV). We need to understand we do not rest in our own completed works but in YeHoVaH's 's finished work. Obtaining separateness (*holiness*), we must abide in Yeshua, the living Word of our Father. In Him, we are empowered to honor His Word through the daily choices we make. As Scripture says, *"Choose you this day whom ye will serve"* (***Joshua 24:15*** KJV), for our decisions reveal the One we are deeply committed to. We receive separateness (*holiness*) by honoring Him through the Torah, divine appointments and obeying His commandments. This includes the fourth commandment, which begins with the word "Remember," a word that underscores the importance of the

Sabbath, *"Remember the sabbath day, to keep it holy"* (***Exodus 20:8*** KJV).

The command to "Remember" is unique, as it is the only commandment that begins with this word. This is where we begin to understand the purpose of the Father keeping a *Book of Remembrance*, as we read in ***Malachi 3:16*** KJV: *"Then they that feared [YeHoVaH] the LORD spake often one to another: and [YeHoVaH] the LORD hearkened, and heard it, and a book of remembrance was written before him for them that feared [YeHoVaH] the LORD, and that thought upon his name."* In ***Deuteronomy 5:15*** KJV, YeHoVaH commands us to *"Observe the sabbath day, to keep it holy [set apart], as [YeHoVaH] the LORD thy God hath commanded thee."*

Sabbath-observance is not just for today but will continue in the new earth. ***Isaiah 66:23*** WEB declares, *"It shall happen that from one new moon to another, and from one sabbath to another, all flesh will come to worship before me," says [YeHoVaH].* This commandment is still a key part of our commitment to separateness (*holiness*), both now and in eternity.

Shabbat and Yeshua, the Messiah

Did you know that Yeshua kept the Sabbath? ***Luke 4:16*** KJV states, *"... And as His custom was, He went into the synagogue on the sabbath day and stood up for to read."* Yeshua Himself kept the Sabbath, showing us by example that it is a day to be set apart for worship and reflection. He even healed on the Sabbath, showing its true purpose of restoration and life (***Mark 3:1-6*** KJV). In ***Matthew 12:8*** KJV, Yeshua declared, *"For the Son of man is [Yeshua] Lord even of the sabbath."* This profound statement affirms His authority over the Sabbath and reminds us that the day is a gift from Him, meant for our benefit and connection with the Father.

Yeshua commanded us to learn from Him and follow His example, saying in *Matthew 11:28-29* WEB *"Come to me, all you who labor and are heavily burdened, and I will give you rest. Take my yoke upon you, and learn from me; for I am gentle and humble in heart; and you will find rest for your souls."* He did not come to abolish the Sabbath, which is also the fourth commandment, but rather fill the Torah to overflowing, abundantly. He came to show us the true spirit of the [*Torah*] law, bringing life, joy, blessings and rest to those who obey it.

Yeshua reminded us that we should never forget and always strive to keep the commandments. *Matthew 5:19* KJV says, *"Whosoever therefore shall break one of these least commandments, and shall teach men so, he shall be called the least in the kingdom of heaven: but whosoever shall do and teach them, the same shall be called great in the kingdom of heaven."* The only way to show and prove our love toward YeHoVaH is by obeying all His commandments: *"For this is loving God, that we keep his commandments. His commandments are not grievous,"* and *"This is love, that we should walk according to his commandments. This is the commandment, even as you heard from the beginning, that you should walk in it"* (*1 John 5:3, 2 John 1:6* WEB). Do not be a Pharisee or Sadducee and make men's traditions of greater value than YeHoVaH's Word because you will become sad you see! Apostle Paul clearly says in *Colossians 2:8* CJB *"Watch out, so that no one will take you captive by means of philosophy and empty deceit, following human tradition which accords with the elemental spirits of the world but does not accord with the Messiah."*

Satan, the enemy of the soul, looks to keep us in bondage to sin as told in **John 8:34** WEB *"[Yeshua] Jesus answered them, Most certainly I tell you, everyone who commits sin is the bound servant of sin."* He does not want us to have a relationship with YeHoVaH , as **Isaiah 59:2** KJV warns, *"But your iniquities have separated between you and your God, and your sins have hid his face from you, that he will not hear."* Satan is no longer outside of the church but orchestrates from within, deceiving humanity through the traditions of men. *"... These people honor me with their lips, but their hearts are far away from me. Their worship of me is useless, because they teach man-made rules as if they were doctrines. You depart from God's command and hold onto human tradition. Indeed, he said to them, you have made fine art of departing from God's command in order to keep your tradition"* (**Mark 7:6-9** CJB).

What the Father has put in place and commanded from the beginning is permanent and eternal. He has not changed His Word, but man has altered it to suit his desires. The Sabbath was never intended to be a burden but a blessing and delight. Yeshua is the fulfillment of that blessing as He invites us, *"Come to me, all you who labor and are heavily burdened, and I will give you rest. Take my yoke upon you and learn from me, for I am gentle and humble in heart; and you will find rest for your souls"* (**Matthew 11:28-29** WEB).

If you profess to be a child and follower of YeHoVaH, then there is still a Sabbath rest for the people of God, as **Hebrews 4:9-11** CJB proclaims: *"So there remains a Shabbat-keeping for God's people. For the one who has entered God's rest has also rested from his own works, as God did from his. Therefore, let us do our best to enter that rest; so that no one will fall short because of the same kind of disobedience."* By entering Shabbat each week and ceasing from your own productivity, you are being obedient to what the Father instituted from the beginning of creation.

This is where the physical and spiritual aspects of Shabbat align, becoming prophetic. Shabbat not only refers back to creation but also points to the Kingdom to come. It celebrates the works of the Father that have already been carried out and predicts the glorious works yet to come. Through Shabbat, we find rest for our souls because Yeshua is our Redeemer, our *Shalom (peace)*, as **Romans 5:11** CJB, says, *"And not only will be delivered in the future, but we are boasting about God right now, because he has acted through our Lord Yeshua the Messiah, through whom we have already received that reconciliation."*

A Foretaste of the Kingdom to Come

As we observe Shabbat, we experience a divine foretaste of the coming Kingdom of YeHoVaH. The Sabbath is not just a weekly rest but a prophetic reminder of the eternal rest that awaits all who are faithful to His commandments. In the book of Hebrews we are told, *"There remaineth therefore a rest to the people of God. For he that is entered into his rest, he also hath ceased from his own works, as [YeHoVaH]God did from His"* (**Hebrews 4:9-10** KJV). This rest is not merely physical but spiritual, a taste of the eternal peace that will come with the Kingdom of YeHoVaH.

The Sabbath reminds us that God's plan for His people includes an eternal rest that will be fully realized in His Kingdom. As **Isaiah 66:22** KJV prophesies, *"For as the new heavens and the new earth, which I will make, shall remain before me, saith [YeHoVaH] the LORD, so shall your seed and your name remain."* The new heaven and new earth are an eternal promise; our weekly observance of Shabbat serves as a symbol of the rest and peace we will experience in that future. *"From new moon to new moon, and from Shabbat to Shabbat, all flesh shall come to worship before me, declares [YeHoVaH] the Lord"* (**Isaiah 66:23** ESV).

Yeshua Himself, when speaking of the future Kingdom, tells us that it is a time of celebration and joy. *"I say to you that many [Gentiles] will come from east and west, and will sit down [start to feast at the table, and enjoy God's promises] with Abraham, Isaac, and Jacob in the kingdom of heaven [because they accepted Me as Savior]"* (**Matthew 8:11** AMP). This kingdom is a place where all who are faithful will find fellowship, peace and rest.

Through the observance of the Sabbath, we are reminded that the Kingdom of YeHoVaH is already here in part, yet to be fully revealed. This weekly rest is a tangible experience of the peace and joy that will be fully realized when His Kingdom comes. In that day, swords will become plowshares (**Isaiah 2:4** KJV), the wolf also shall dwell with the lamb…and a little child shall lead them (**Isaiah 11:6** KJV) and **Revelation 21:4** KJV offers this promise, *"And [YeHoVaH] God shall wipe away all tears from their eyes; and there shall be no more death, neither sorrow, nor crying, neither shall there be any more pain: for the former things are passed away."* The Kingdom of YeHoVaH will be one of total restoration, where all suffering and pain will cease and we will enter everlasting joy.

As we celebrate Shabbat, we not only rest from our labors but also anticipate the coming rest that will be eternal. We look forward to the day when, as **Revelation 22:3-5** CJB declares, *"…no longer will there be any curses. The throne of God and of the Lamb will be in the city, and his servants will worship him; they will see his face, and his name will be on their foreheads. Night will no longer exist, so they will need* *neither the light of the lamp nor the light of the sun, because [YeHoVaH] ADONAI, God, will shine upon them. And they will reign as kings forever and ever."* This is the ultimate fulfillment of the Sabbath, a rest that begins in this life and finds its culmination in the eternal Kingdom of YeHoVaH.

As we observe the Sabbath, we are given a foretaste of the joy, peace and rest that will be ours in the Kingdom to come. As we honor this day, we are not only keeping a commandment but also taking part in the divine anticipation of the eternal rest promised to all of YeHoVaH's people. Until that day, Shabbat is our prophetic pause, a time where heaven touches earth in our homes, our hearts and our families.

More Than a Day Off

In today's culture, people often confuse rest with entertainment or escape. True rest is not found in watching more shows or scrolling more screens. It is found in YeHoVaH's presence. The Sabbath is a divine gift meant to draw us closer to Him and deepen our relationship with our Creator. In Exodus, we are reminded to remember the Sabbath and keep it holy, ceasing from our usual labor and focusing on the things of the Kingdom of YeHoVaH. It is a time to stop working, start worshiping, celebrate our identity, receive spiritual reflection and renewal, rest in Him and trust in His provision.

Yeshua Himself modeled the true purpose of the Sabbath, teaching that it was made for man's benefit, not as a burden but as a blessing. As we rest on this day, we acknowledge that our provision and strength come from Him and true peace and rest are found in obedience to His commandments.

Our labor is not in vain; the Sabbath points us to the rest that is yet to come, an eternal rest in His presence.

Thus, the Sabbath is more than just a day off; it is a set apart time that renews our spirit, strengthens our faith and reminds us of the rest that awaits in the Kingdom of YeHoVaH. It is a day of separateness (*holiness*) to draw near to Him, find Shalom (*peace*) in His presence and honor His commandments. It is not about legalism; it is about an invitation. Yehovah is saying, "Come be with Me. Let Me remind you of who you are. Let Me bless your family, fill your home and pour My Shalom (*peace*) upon your soul."

Shabbat Resistance

In a world that values productivity and success, keeping Shabbat is an act of faith. It reminds us that we do not need to prove ourselves or constantly strive. For one day, we rest in the knowledge that we belong to YeHoVaH, who provides, protects and gives us peace.

Shabbat is a refuge, resisting the world's demands and offering us a pause from the noise of daily life. It centers our hearts and reminds us of our true source. In a culture that worships speed and achievement, Shabbat is a choice to stop and rest in His presence, free from the pressure to perform.

As we observe Shabbat, we push back against the workload, anxiety and spiritual forgetfulness that consume us. It is a time to recalibrate our hearts and realign with YeHoVaH's rhythm. We are reminded that our worth is not in what we do but to whom we belong.

Shabbat teaches us that we do not need to be constantly working or achieving. Instead, we embrace the completeness we have in Him. It is a surrender to His peace and a declaration of our dependence on YeHoVaH, rejecting the world's view of success.

Reflection Questions

1. Do you see Shabbat as a spiritual experience or just a day off?
2. How does Shabbat reflect your covenant relationship with YeHoVaH?
3. What would it look like for you to make Shabbat a "prophetic pause" in your life?

Declaration

Father, help me to enter your complete rest, not through my own works but through Your covenant. I receive the peace, presence and power of Shabbat. My soul delights in You, YeHoVaH, and my spirit rejoices in Your Son, Yeshua, the Messiah of the Sabbath. I surrender to Your rhythm and trust in Your provision, knowing that in Your rest, I am renewed and complete. May Your peace fill my heart and Your presence refresh my soul as I honor and worship You on this set apart day. Amen

Reader Review: *"The Gift of Shabbat by Scott and Amanda Cumbee is an excellent source that provides absolute truth with Biblical references of the Creator's expectations in remembering and keeping the Sabbath.* **The Gift of Shabbat** *is also a family friendly source that shows the importance and inclusion of each family member in working together to keep the true Shabbat instead of just keeping tradition." By: Adam and LeAnn, Retired Teachers*

Chapter 5
Preparing for Shabbat: Welcoming the King with Joy

"On the sixth day they gathered twice as much bread, two omers for each one" (***Exodus 16:22*** KJV).

Shabbat does not begin when the candles are lit or when the sun sets, it begins with preparation. In Scripture, we read that the Israelites were to gather a double portion of manna on the sixth day, so that they could rest on the seventh. This day of preparation "Eve of Shabbat" is not just about chores or coordination. It is an act of honor. It says, **"The King is coming. Let us get ready!"**

When we prepare for Shabbat, we are not merely setting a table but making room for glory.

The Sixth Day: A Day of Anticipation

On Friday, the sixth day is filled with joyful expectancy. It is a consecrated rhythm where families prepare the home and their hearts for the arrival of Shabbat as if welcoming a royal guest. Every detail from the food to the atmosphere becomes part of the invitation. It is a wonderful gift from the Father.

Exodus 16:23 CJB reminds us that Shabbat rest needs foresight.

He told them, "This is what [YeHoVaH] ADONAI has said: 'Tomorrow is a holy Shabbat for [YeHoVaH] ADONAI. Bake what you want to bake; and boil what you want to boil; and whatever is left over, set aside and keep for the morning."

This teaches us that rest must be prepared for; it does not happen by accident. It is an act of discipline and joy.

Our preparation for Shabbat truly begins in the middle of the week. For example, the sourdough challah bread we serve on Shabbat is started on Wednesday and completed on Thursday. During these days, we also tend to practical matters such as laundry, fresh linens and cleaning the bathrooms. If there is yard work to be done, we aim to finish it by Thursday as well.

We also do our best to prepare foods ahead of time, especially desserts and other dishes that can be made in advance, so that Friday is not rushed. Each step of preparation is an act of setting apart our home, making it ready to welcome the peace and separateness (*holiness*) of Shabbat.

This is how we personally make our household ready to honor and receive Shabbat.

1. The Home: Clean and Clothed in Honor

A clean environment sets the atmosphere for honor. Our family:

- Sweep and vacuum the floors
- Take out the trash
- Set out special dishes used only for Shabbat
- Last minute - cooking, washing dishes, wipe down kitchen and make sure the dishwasher is empty for our plates to be set in after our Shabbat meal

This preparation is not about striving for perfection; it is about cultivating a posture of the heart. A clean and orderly home becomes a reflection of a spirit that longs to welcome the peace of YeHoVaH into every room. As we often say in the South, "cleanliness is next to Godliness," and in the rhythm of Shabbat, this truth takes on a deeper meaning. Our outward readiness mirrors the inward desire to honor Him and make space for His presence to dwell.

2. The Table: Set for an Encounter

The Shabbat table is more than a place to share a meal; it is like an altar set apart to welcome the presence of YeHoVaH. Every item has meaning and helps us prepare for an encounter (*all are optional except bread and wine/juice*).

- **Candleholders** - to welcome the light of Shabbat
- **Two Candles** - representing both creation and covenant
- **Menorah** - reminding us that Yeshua, the Light of the World, shines forth in the fullness of the seven Spirits of God, bringing His fire and presence into our rest
- **Kiddush Cup** - a special cup set apart for the blessing over the wine or grape juice
- **Wine Glasses** - for each person at the table to share in the Kiddush blessing together
- **Challah Board/Plate with Cover** - holding the two loaves, symbolizing the double portion of manna
- **White Cloth** - covering the challah, a picture of the hidden manna in the wilderness
- **Special Dishes** - plates, bowls and silverware reserved only for Shabbat
- **Serving Trays and Utensils** - for the meal prepared in honor of the day
- **Flowers** - bringing beauty and joy to the table as a reflection of Shabbat's delight

Everything on the table tells a story. It invites the family to see, taste and remember.

3. The Meals: Prepared in Peace

Cooking before Shabbat is a loving act. The meals do not have to be gourmet; they just need to be ready before sundown. Traditionally, one meal is shared on Friday night and one on Saturday, often with leftovers or simple foods so no labor is needed.

In many homes, Friday night dinner is a set apart time, a gathering filled with blessings, laughter and presence. It is a feast that celebrates not only YeHoVaH's provision but His people.

4. The Heart: Quieted and Expectant

True preparation for Shabbat goes beyond setting the table or finishing the chores; it is about preparing the heart. Before the candles are lit and the blessings are spoken, pause and enter stillness. This is where we step into the secret place with YeHoVaH, drawing near to Him in separateness (*holiness*) and rest.

Take a moment in stillness to:

- **Repent** of any sin, burdens or heaviness carried from the week.
- **Lay down** every unfinished task, trusting YeHoVaH to provide.
- **Refresh your body** by taking a bath and putting on clean clothing, allowing the outward to reflect the purity of YeHoVaH working inward.
- **Invite His reign** over the next 24 hours, welcoming His *Shalom* (*peace*) and presence into your home and heart.

Here, we shift from chaos of the world to the harmony of God's order, from the burden of striving to the calmness of His presence. It is a divine exchange, our striving for His peace and our weariness for His rest. As you quiet your spirit, invite Ruach HaKodesh (*Set Apart Spirit*, *The Holy Spirit*) to consecrate your thoughts, renew your emotions and prepare you for a divine encounter.

5. The Family: Aligned and United

Shabbat is a gift of blessing for the whole family. When everyone prepares and takes part together, unity is cultivated and the presence of YeHoVaH is magnified in the home. The table becomes a place of encounter, not just with one another but with the Father, King of the Universe.

Your Shabbat may look different in practice, but Scripture gives us clear requirements to honor the day as separate. You are free to shape your own family traditions or draw from what others have done. Nonetheless, there are opportunities for you to create ways to enrich but never replace what God has commanded. Our family-centered Shabbat looks similar to this:

- **Children help with preparation** - setting the table, arranging flowers or helping with the candles
- **The Shofar is blown** - marking the entrance into sacred time and announcing Shabbat's arrival
- **Candles are lit before sunset** - welcoming the Light of Shabbat and inviting His peace to rest on the home
- **Scripture is read aloud** - by children, parents or even guests, so that the Word fills the atmosphere
- **Spouses pray over each other or together** - asking for peace, intimacy and the strengthening of their covenant

- **Parents bless their children** - speaking life, identity and destiny over them
- **Worship music** - lifts hearts in gratitude and joy
- **The meal is shared** - communion and then enjoying the fruits of the week's labor in rest and celebration
- **Fathers (or spiritual leaders) share lessons** - imparting wisdom and faith to the next generation

In this rhythm, Shabbat becomes more than a weekly routine; it becomes a generational inheritance. Each moment of preparation and participation trains children to honor YeHoVaH's rhythm of rest and to carry His presence into the future generations.

Common Shabbat Prep Checklist

[Please keep in mind that your checklist may not look like this and it is totally fine. Not everyone's home is the same or have the same chores. Just use this as a guide to make your own checklist.]

Home Prepared

- House cleaned
- Laundry done
- Linens fresh
- Yard work finished

Table Set for an Encounter

- Candleholders
- Two candles
- Menorah
- Kiddush cup
- Wine glasses
- Challah board/plate with cover
- Two loaves of challah
- White cloth

- Special dishes and silverware
- Serving trays and utensils
- Flowers

Meals Prepared

- Challah baked
- Desserts prepared
- Main meal ready (enough for the next day as well/or something prepared different from main meal)

The Heart: Quieted and Expectant

- Repent
- Release tasks
- Bath taken
- Clean clothing put on
- Invite YeHoVaH to reign
- Enter the secret place

The Family: Aligned and United

- Children help prepare
- Shofar blown
- Candles lit
- Scripture read aloud
- Spouses pray together
- Parents bless children
- Worship music
- Meal enjoyed
- Father/leader shares lessons

The Joy of Anticipation

Psalm 92 KJV, the song for the Sabbath day, begins with these words: *"It is good to give thanks to [YeHoVaH] the LORD, and to sing praises unto thy name, O Most High."*

Shabbat is not something we stumble into weary and empty; it is something we run toward with joy and expectation. Every act of preparation is worship itself, a motion of faith declaring: **"I am ready to meet with You."**

Find a Shabbat song that stirs your spirit, one that feels like more than a melody, something that carries the weight of separateness (*holiness*) and the joy of the Father's presence. When your family sings it together, it becomes movement, hands lifted, hearts opened and voices joined in harmony with heaven. It is not just a song; it is an offering.

When you treat Shabbat like a treasure, your family will come to cherish it. It becomes the anchor of the week, the time and place where YeHoVaH speaks, heals and restores.

Reflection Question

> If you could describe the "joy of anticipation" of Shabbat in one word, what would it be?

Reader Review: *"Shabbat is truly a day of worship and a time I treasure deeply with my family. Around the table, we eat, laugh and play games together, enjoying both fellowship and rest. As we open the Scriptures, they come alive in such a special way, filling our home with peace and joy. This book is one everyone should read. It carries a message that is timely and full of blessing. Through it, I realized that Shabbat is more than just sharing a meal; it's dining with the King Himself." By Faith, Student and Sabbath Keeper*

Chapter 6
Welcoming the Sabbath: Entering His Rest with Light and Blessing

"If you turn away your foot from the Sabbath, from doing your pleasure on My [set apart] holy day, and call the Sabbath a delight... then you shall delight yourself in [YeHoVaH] the LORD"
(***Isaiah 58:13-14*** KJV).

The Sabbath does not arrive quietly, it enters like a bride adorned for her husband, like a queen stepping into her courts. Friday evening as the sun begins to set, the atmosphere changes. It feels like time slows down and heaven begins to draw near. The work has ceased, the table is prepared and now it is time to welcome the King, YeHoVaH.

This is not merely a tradition; it is a set apart (*holy*) encounter. The Sabbath is a consecrated day set up by YeHoVaH at creation, a set apart time for all humanity as a gift of rest and communion. When we welcome Shabbat in on Friday evening at sunset, we are not just observing a practice, we are opening the doors of our homes and the gates of our hearts to Yeshua, (*salvation*) the LORD of the Sabbath, to dwell with us in His peace and presence.

Celebrating the Gift of Shabbat

Shabbat is not about rituals or endless rules. It is about honoring the covenant rest that YeHoVaH established from the beginning. Scripture gives us what is necessary.

These are the anchors of Shabbat. They will never change.

- Rest from ordinary work (***Exodus 20:9-10***)
- Remember the Sabbath and keep it holy (***Exodus 20:8; Deuteronomy 5:12***)
- Assemble in fellowship, a holy convocation (***Leviticus 23:3***)

Around the world, families celebrate Shabbat in many different ways. Some light candles, share songs or blessings, while others focus on Scripture readings and prayer. Each practice has a story, meaning and reason why certain families choose to include it in their service. These expressions are not commanded but they can enrich the experience of Shabbat for those who find them meaningful.

The simplicity of Shabbat brings out the beauty of worship and honors the Father. Some elements will speak more deeply to one household than to another. One family may hold fast to a particular expression, while another emphasizes something different. There is nothing wrong with this, as long as everything flows back to the purpose of honoring YeHoVaH's Sabbath.

In this book, we have given you the Scriptures and shown you exactly what the Word says. This is the beauty of our Father; He allows you to set your table, prepare a meal and honor Him together.

As you look around your table at your family and friends you will see the goodness of YeHoVaH. He has brought people in your life so that you might share the gift of Shabbat. Even the stranger, widow and orphan are welcomed; He has blessed you to be a blessing.

Keep the focus on what is necessary. While the expressions may differ, the heart of it all remains the same. It is worshiping YeHoVaH together in unity on His set apart day.

The Beauty of Erev Shabbat

"Erev" means evening and Erev Shabbat marks Friday night, the true beginning of the biblical day, as written in (**Genesis 1:5** KJV): *"And there was evening, and there was morning..."* This is the moment Shabbat begins, not with heaviness or ritual but with light, song and blessing.

The heart of Erev Shabbat is simple, yet profound:

- Cease from your labor and rest in Him
- Remember your identity as His chosen people, "For many are called (*invited, summoned*), but few are chosen" (**Matthew 22:14** AMP)
- Honor the One who alone gives true rest

It is a joyous time to lay down the burdens of the week and to welcome YeHoVaH's presence. Around the table family and friends celebrate His goodness, His provision and His covenant love. In this glorious rhythm, every Friday evening at sunset becomes a doorway into Shabbat's *Shalom* (*peace*), beauty and delight.

The Order of Welcoming Shabbat

The order of Erev Shabbat in the home is both consecrated and flexible. Tradition offers a beautiful framework, yet each family is invited to make it their own, through prayers, blessings, songs and worship. The heart of Shabbat is not rigid formality; the true essence is honoring YeHoVaH and welcoming His presence.

Shabbat is more than a weekly pause; it is a divine rehearsal. Each week prepare and enter rest, practicing for the greater rest to come. There is a wedding feast awaiting with Yeshua, our Bridegroom and one day we will dwell with Him forever. Each Shabbat whispers that the King is coming. Search your heart to see how you are preparing for his arrival.

When you gather, bless and rest in Him, it is being inscribed into His Book of Remembrance. This rhythm aligns you with His Word and teaches to yearn for His Kingdom. Shabbat is not only about rest but also about readiness.

Use this Shabbat book as a guideline but remember as the reality of Shabbat becomes more alive to you each week, you may be led by *Ruach HaKodesh* (*Set Apart Spirit, The Holy Spirit*) to add your own prayers and expressions of worship. Let the Spirit of YeHoVaH direct your preparation and celebration so His presence becomes your delight and joy.

1. Lighting the Candles

In many homes, the woman lights the Shabbat candles as a way of ushering in peace and holiness; yet a man may do so as well, since this is a custom of honor not a command of Scripture. *[Traditionally, the lady or mother of the home will light two candles. They are lit before the sun sets (usually 18-20 minutes before) to signify the two commands given on the Sabbath to remember it and keep it holy (set apart). Yeshua has sanctified us by His blood.]*

- Creation and Redemption
- Remember and Observe (*Zachor* and *Shamor*)

When YeHoVaH gave the Ten Commandments, two different words were spoken concerning Shabbat:

- Zachor -" ז Remember" (***Exodus 20:8***): "*Remember the Sabbath day, to keep it holy.*"
  This means to call Shabbat to mind, treasure it and set

it apart as a divine encounter. Remembering is an act of the heart. It is cherishing the covenant and recalling that YeHoVaH is our Creator and Deliverer.
- Shamor - "Observe" (***Deuteronomy 5:12***): *"Observe the Sabbath day, to keep it holy, as [YeHoVaH] the Lord your God commanded you."*
  This means to guard, keep watch over and actively live out Shabbat. Observing is an act of the will. It is how to keep it consecrated through actions by resting, ceasing from labor and entering His presence.

2. Blowing the Shofar
[Your family and friends might enjoy blowing the shofar as welcoming the Sabbath also. Children find this especially fun.]

3. Opening Prayer
[Mother or Lady of the home recites the following prayer. Daughters may also join in. If no women are present, the father or another family member may lead in welcoming Shabbat.]

Hebrew Translation
Ba-ruch at-tah YeHoVaH, E-lo-hei-nu me-lekh ha-o-lam, a-sher kid-sha-nu b-dam Yeshua. V-tzi-va-nu l-hi-yot or l-o-lam.

English Translation
Blessed are you, YeHoVaH, our God, King of the Universe, who sanctified us by the blood of Yeshua and commanded us to be a light to the nations.

Shabbat Shalom Everyone!
Welcome Shabbat with a Song of Praise!

4. The Sabbath Day

[The Dad or the Leader of the home will read the following Scriptures that comes from the Torah. Family and guest may read along with the Dad or Leader to themselves.]

"On the seventh day God was finished with his work which he had made, so he rested on the seventh day from all his work which he had made" (**Genesis 2:2** CJB).

Tell the people of Israel, you are to observe my Shabbats; for this is a sign between me and you through all your generations; so that you will know that I am [YeHoVaH] ADONAI, who sets you apart for me. Therefore you are to keep my Sabbath because it is set apart for you. Everyone who treats it as ordinary must be put to death; for whoever does any work on it is to be cut off from his people. On six days work will get done; but the seventh day is Shabbat, for complete rest, set apart for [YeHoVaH] ADONAI. Whoever does any work on the day of Shabbat must be put to death. The people of Israel are to keep the Shabbat, to observe Shabbat through all their generations as a perpetual covenant. It is a sign between me and the people of Israel forever; for in six days [YeHoVaH] ADONAI made heaven and earth, but on the seventh day He stopped working and rested" (**Exodus 31:13-17** CJB).

Work is to be done on six days. The seventh day is a *Sabbath* of complete rest, a divine convocation. You are not to do any kind of work; it is a *Shabbat* for YeHoVaH, even in your homes. This is YeHoVaH's redemption program to meet with His redeemed people, a weekly appointment. Shabbat was created before the giving of the Torah [*the Father's instruction*]. It means to rest or sit down. *"For six days work may be done, but the seventh day is the Sabbath a complete rest, a holy convocation (calling together). You shall not do any work [on that day]; it is the Sabbath of [YeHoVaH] the LORD wherever you may be"* (***Leviticus 23:3*** AMP).

For in six days, YeHoVaH made heaven and earth, the sea and everything in them but on the seventh day He rested. This is why YeHoVaH blessed the day, *Shabbat* and separated it for himself (***Exodus 20:8-11***).

Father and Dad in Shabbat Blessings
When Yeshua said, *"And call no man your father on earth, for you have one Father, who is in heaven"* (***Matthew 23:9*** ESV). He was warning against giving men the reverence and authority that belongs only to YeHoVaH. Yet throughout Scripture, the word *father* is used rightly and honorably. Abraham is called *Father Abraham* (***Luke 16:24***) and Paul spoke of himself as a father in the faith (***1 Corinthians 4:15***). On Shabbat, when a dad blesses his family, he is not replacing the Heavenly Father but serving as a vessel for YeHoVaH. For this reason, we may call it the "father's blessing" in the sense that YeHoVaH's love flows through the earthly dad to his children. This way, the title honors both roles, the Heavenly Father as the source and the earthly dad as the channel.

5. Family Dynamic Application
*[Shabbat is YeHoVaH's covenant sign with us. By keeping Shabbat, we are acknowledging His creation of our reality in six days. Yeshua states in **John 14:15** KJV, "if you love me, keep my commandments. So, **Deuteronomy 6:1-3, 6-9, 20-25** is a wonderful way to begin with your family.]*

Leader
[The father or man of the home, may read these words or he may choose another individual to read.]

Now this is the *mitzvah* (*commandment*), the laws and rulings which [*YeHoVaH*] *ADONAI* your God ordered me to teach you for you to obey in the land you are crossing over to possess, so that you will fear [*YeHoVaH*] *ADONAI* your God and observe all His regulations and *mitzvot* (*commandments*) that I am giving you - you, your child and your grandchild - as long as you live, and so that you will have long life. Therefore listen, Isra´el, and take care to obey, so that things will go well with you, and so that you will increase greatly, as [*YeHoVaH*] *ADONAI*, the God of your ancestors, promised you by giving you a land flowing with milk and honey (**Deuteronomy 6:1-3** CJB). These words, which I am ordering you today, are to be on your heart; and you are to teach them carefully to your children. You are to talk about them when you sit at home, when you are traveling on the road, when you lie down and when you get up. Tie them on your hand as a sign, put them at the front of a headband around your forehead, and write them on the doorframes of your house and on your gates (**Deuteronomy 6:6-9** CJB). Some day your child will ask you, "What is the meaning of the [*Torah*] instructions, laws and rulings which [*YeHoVaH*] *ADONAI* our God has laid down for you?" Then you will tell your child, "We were slaves to Pharaoh in Egypt, and [*YeHoVaH*] *ADONAI* brought us out of Egypt with a strong hand. [*YeHoVaH*] *ADONAI* worked great and terrible signs and wonders against Egypt, Pharaoh and all his household, before our very eyes. He brought us out from there in order to bring us to the land he had sworn to our ancestors that he would give us. [*YeHoVaH*] *ADONAI* ordered us to observe all these laws [*Torah*], to fear [*YeHoVaH*] *ADONAI* our God, always for our own good, so that he might keep us alive, as we are today. It will be righteousness for us if we are careful to obey all these *mitzvot (commandments)* before [*YeHoVaH*] *ADONAI* our God, just as he ordered us to do" (**Deuteronomy 6:20-25** CJB).

6. The Avinu's Prayer
[A Prayer To Our Father: Hebrew Origins Of The LORD's Prayer, By Dr. Nehemia Gordon and Keith Johnson]

Together: Everyone Reads

Our Father in heaven, may your name YeHoVaH be sanctified. May your kingdom be blessed. Your will shall be done in heaven and on earth. Give us our bread continually. Forgive us the debt of our sins as we forgive the debt of those who sin against us. Do not bring us into the hands of a test and protect us from all evil. Amen

Song: *Your choice of praise and worship*

7. Blessing Over the Wife
*[This consecrated blessing is spoken by the husband and children over the wife and mother. The couple begins by facing one another, as the children look on. In this moment, the husband humbles himself before YeHoVaH and before his family, taking his wife's hand or gently laying his hand upon her to declare the living Word of YeHoVaH over her life. Together the family recites portions of **Proverbs 31:10–31**, the timeless passage that exalts the virtuous woman, a mighty warrior. After the father leads, he invites the children to join with him in proclaiming the final verses, so that the mother is surrounded by the voices of her husband and children blessing her. This act not only honors the mother as the heart of the home but also acknowledges her as a vessel of wisdom, strength and legacy. It is a moment of thanksgiving for the gift of her life and devotion and a reminder that her worth is far above rubies.]*

Husband/Father
[Decrees this blessing over his wife]

Father, I thank You for the gift of Your favor in blessing our home with a truly virtuous and excellent wife.

Wife's name: _____, you are far more valuable than jewels. My heart trusts in you completely and you enrich my life every day. You bring me good, not harm, all the days of your life.

Wife's name: _____, you extend your hands to the poor and your arms are open wide to the needy. Strength and dignity are your covering; you smile at the future without fear. When you open your mouth, wisdom flows; the teaching of kindness is always on your tongue. You watch faithfully over our household, never walking in idleness.

Children (together with their father):
We rise up and call you happy and blessed! We declare with joy, "Many women have done excellently but you surpass them all!" Charm is deceptive and beauty fades but because you fear Yehovah, you will be praised forever. We honor you for all that you have done; your works will proclaim your praise at the gates.

8. Blessing Over the Husband
[This consecrated blessing is spoken by the wife which represents the crown of her husband as they continue to stand or sit facing one another. In this divine moment, the children witness their mother humbling herself before YeHoVaH and before the family, honoring her husband as the priest and leader of the home. With love and reverence, she takes his hand and declares the living Word of YeHoVaH over his life, speaking forth promises of strength, righteousness and prosperity. This blessing becomes a

testimony to the children, showing them how a wife partners with YeHoVaH in prayer and honor, covering her husband with scripture and affirming his role in the covenant of their home. What a beautiful and powerful blessing!]

Husband's Name: _____, how joyful is the man who fears YeHoVaH, who delights in His commandments. Your descendants will be mighty upon the earth, a blessed generation of the upright shall arise after you. Wealth and riches are in your house; your righteousness endures forever. To the upright you shine as a light in the darkness. You are merciful, compassionate and righteous. Things go well for you as you deal mercifully and lend. You handle your affairs with fairness; surely you will never be moved. The righteous man will be remembered forever. You will not be shaken by evil tidings, for your heart is steadfast, trusting in YeHoVaH. What man desires life and loves many days, that he may see good?

Husband's Name: _____, keep your tongue from evil and your lips from deceitful speech; turn away from evil and do good. Seek peace and pursue it! The steps of a righteous man are ordered by YeHoVaH and He delights in your way. Though you stumble, you will not fall headlong, for YeHoVaH upholds you with His hand. Mark the blameless man and behold the upright, for the man of peace will have a future and a legacy.

Blessed are you, **Husband's Name:** _____, for you do not walk in the counsel of the ungodly, nor stand in the way of sinners, nor sit in the seat of mockers. Your delight is in the Torah of YeHoVaH and in His Torah you meditate day and night. You are like a tree firmly planted by rivers of living water that brings forth its fruit in season, whose leaf does not wither and whatever you do shall prosper.

(***Psalm 112:1–3, 5–7; Psalm 34:12–14; Psalm 37:23–24, 37; Psalm 1:1–3***)

9. Blessing Over the Children
[This beautiful tradition speaks identity and destiny over each child. In this divine moment, the father gathers his children nearby. He may choose to go to each one individually, laying his hands upon their heads to release the blessing of YeHoVaH. As he does this, he stands in the role of the High Priest of his home, modeling the heart of Yeshua who blesses His children. This weekly act is more than tradition, it is a declaration of faith, hope and encouragement that prepares the children for the week ahead and roots them deeply in the covenant love of YeHoVaH.]

Father to Sons
My son, may you walk in the footsteps of the patriarchs like Abraham in faith, Isaac in discernment and Jacob in praise (***Hebrews 11:8–21***).

May YeHoVaH bless you with the blessing of Ephraim and Manasseh (***Genesis 48:20***), forgetting the pain of your past and living fruitfully every day of your life. May YeHoVaH prepare you to become a Godly husband and father. May He bring to you a virtuous wife who will walk beside you in covenant forever. May your strength be proven in righteousness and your name be remembered with honor in the house of YeHoVaH.

Father to Daughters
My daughter, may you reflect the beauty and strength of the matriarchs like Sarah in faith (***Hebrews 11:11***), Rebecca in kindness (***Genesis 24:19***), Rachel and Leah in building the household of Israel (***Ruth 4:11***).

May YeHoVaH bless you with virtue and compassion, clothing you with strength and dignity. May He grant you long life filled with joy and bring to you a husband that will be the priest of your house covering you and your children while cherishing, protecting and honoring you. May YeHoVaH surround you with peace and establish your home as a wellspring of blessing for generations to come.

10. Parents' Blessing Over the Children
[In the warmth of Shabbat, father and mother together lift their voices to speak a blessing over their children. With hands laid gently and hearts full of love, they declare the promises of YeHoVaH, reminding their sons and daughters that His Word is life, peace and guidance for all their days. This blessing is not only a prayer but also a prophetic declaration that their children will walk in covenant, clothed with grace and truth, rooted in faith and secure in the love of their family and YeHoVaH.]

Parents to Children
My beloved children do not forget my teaching but let your heart keep my commandments. They will add to you length of days, years of life and peace. Do not let grace and truth forsake you; bind them around your neck and write them on the tablet of your heart. So, you will find favor and good understanding in the sight of YeHoVaH and of people.

Trust in YeHoVaH with all your heart. Do not lean unto your own understanding. In all your ways acknowledge Him and He will make your paths straight.

Be not wise in your own eyes; fear YeHoVaH and turn away from evil. It will be healing to your body and strength to your bones (***Proverbs 3:1-8***).

11. The Priestly/Aaronic Blessing
[The Dad or leader of the home will stand to pray this blessing over all the existing members of the home and their guest. This is the blessing YeHoVaH gave to Moses to have his sons bless the Israelites].

Hebrew Translation
Ye-va-re-khe-kha YeHoVaH ve-yish-me-re-kha
Ya´-er YeHoVaH pa-nav e-ley-kha vi-chu-ne-ka
Yi-sa YeHoVaH pa-nav e-ley-kha ve-ya-sem le-kha sha-lom.

English Translation
YeHoVaH bless you and keep you; YeHoVaH make His face to shine upon you and be gracious to you; YeHoVaH lift up His countenance upon you and give you peace.
Shalom (***Numbers 6:24-26*** KJV)

"Ehyeh Asher Ehyeh" I am/will be what I am/will be. (***Exodus 3:14*** CJB)

Song: *Your choice of praise and worship*

12. Sh´ma
[This is a scriptural prayer that is spoken daily by Jewish culture worldwide.]

Together: Everyone Reads

Hebrew Translation
Sh´ma Yisra´el!
YeHoVaH Eloheinu,
YeHoVaH Ech´ad
Baruch Shem
K´vod Malchooto
L´olam Va´ed.

English Translation
Hear O Israel, YeHoVaH our Elohim, YeHoVaH is One (***Deuteronomy 6:4*** KJV). Praise be the name of His Glorious Kingdom Sovereignty forever and ever (***Psalm 92:19*** KJV).

Together: Everyone Reads
And you shall love YeHoVaH, your GOD with all your heart, with all your soul and with all your might. These words which I command you this day shall be upon your heart. You shall teach them thoroughly to your children. You shall speak of them when you sit in your house, walk on the road, lie down and when you rise. You shall bind them for a sign upon your hand; they shall be a reminder between your eyes. You shall write them on the doorposts of your house and upon your gates (***Deuteronomy 6:4-9*** KJV).

13. Prayer for Israel

*[Prayer 1 is a prayer that was first written by the Chief Rabbi of the State of Israel in 1948 and has since been lifted up in synagogues across the world every Shabbat. As grafted-in sons and daughters of Abraham through Messiah Yeshua, we now join in this blessing with joy and reverence, giving thanks for YeHoVaH's covenant people and His promised land (**Deuteronomy 30: 4-5**).*
You may choose to read prayer 2 instead. The choice is yours. The father or leader of the home may read these words or he may choose another individual to read.]

Leader
Beloved family, we have been given the privilege of being grafted into YeHoVaH's household. **Romans 11:23-24** portrays Gentile believers as wild olive shoots grafted into a cultivated olive tree (*Israel*), emphasizing God's power, mercy and the unity of believers through faith. The passage also underscores that natural branches (*Israel*), those originally part of the tree, can be grafted back if they turn from unbelief. Let us remember that Israel is not only a land but the heritage of YeHoVaH's people. As we pray, we teach our children the significance of aligning our hearts with YeHoVaH's purposes and giving Him praise for the heritage that awaits His family.

Prayer 1
Our Father in Heaven, Protector and Redeemer of Israel, bless the State of Israel which marks the first glimmering of our deliverance. Shield it beneath the wings of Your love; spread it over Your Canopy of peace; send Your light and Your truth to its leaders, officers and counselors and direct them with Your good counsel. O YeHoVaH, strengthen the defenders of our Holy Land; grant them salvation and crown them with victory. Establish peace in the land and everlasting joy for its inhabitants. Remember our brethren, the whole house of Israel, in all the lands of their dispersion. Speedily let them walk upright to Zion, the city, to Jerusalem, Your dwelling place, as it is written in the Torah of Your servant Moses, even if you are dispersed in the uttermost parts of the world, from there YeHoVaH your God will gather and fetch you. YeHoVaH your God will bring you into the land which your fathers possessed and you shall possess it.
Unite our hearts to love and revere Your Name and to observe all the precepts of Your Torah. Shine forth in Your glorious majesty over all the inhabitants of Your world. Let everything that breathes proclaim, "YeHoVaH God of Israel is King; His majesty rules over all." Amen

Prayer 2
Even if you are scattered to the farthest part of heaven, from there YeHoVaH your Elohim will gather you and He will bring you back. He will bring you into the land your fathers possessed and you shall possess it. He will do you good and multiply you more than your fathers (***Deuteronomy 30:4–5***).

Father, we thank You for the land of Israel and for the people whom You have called Your own. We bless Your covenant people; we pray for their peace, restoration and redemption in

Yeshua the Messiah. Gather them from every nation, root them deeply in Your Torah and cause Your light to shine from Zion to the ends of the earth.

We rejoice that, through Yeshua, we too have been grafted into this covenant family. May our children grow up with hearts that love Your land, honor Your people and long for the day when all Israel will be saved. We lift our voices in unity with Israel and the nations, proclaiming:

Together: Everyone Reads

Baruch attah, YeHoVaH, Blessed are You, Yehovah, who is faithful to all His promises!

Song: *Your choice of praise and worship*

14. Handwashing

*[In the Torah, YeHoVaH commanded the priest to wash their hands and feet before ministering in the Tabernacle: "And YeHoVaH spake unto Moses, saying, Thou shalt also make a laver of brass...for Aaron and his sons shall wash their hands and their feet thereat. When they go into the tabernacle of the congregation, they shall wash with water, that they die not" (**Exodus 30:17-21** KJV). This instruction applied only to the priesthood, not to the entire nation of Israel, and it was not tied to Shabbat meals. Some families include it as a beautiful tradition, finding joy in its symbolism. Others do not observe it, choosing instead to go straight to the blessing of the bread. Both practices are acceptable because what YeHoVaH values most is not ritual but obedience as we remember His covenant. If your family chooses to include this tradition, here is a simple way...]*

Leader
[The father or leader carries a bowl of water and towel around the table, serving each guest, beginning with his wife. Each guest dips their right hand, then their left and dries them on the towel. When all are finished, the wife (or first guest served) holds the bowl and towel for the leader.]

As our hands are washed, we declare that through your blood, Yeshua, our sins are removed. We wash outwardly, but Yeshua, You wash us inwardly, making us pure before the Father.
(*Pause for washing*)

Together: Everyone Reads

Blessed are You, YeHoVaH our God, King of the Universe, Who has washed us clean by the power of Ruach HaKodesh (*Set Apart Spirit, The Holy Spirit*), through the completed work of Yeshua the Messiah and has called us to be set apart for Your kingdom and glory. Amen

15. Communion
[As Shabbat draws us into the covenant rest of YeHoVaH, the father or leader of the home now leads the family and guests in the sacred act of communion. This is not a mere ritual but a holy encounter with the living Messiah. Around this table of covenant, hearts are invited into repentance, forgiveness and deliverance. For husbands and fathers, this moment reflects the priesthood of the home as they stand as spiritual coverings, modeling the love and sacrifice of Yeshua for His people.]

Blessing Over the Bread
[During Shabbat, some families include an optional tradition known as the Covenant of Salt. As the challah is being passed around the table, each family member and guest tears off a small piece. Some choose to dip the bread into salt,

*remembering what Scripture calls "the salt of the covenant" (**Leviticus 2:13**). In Scripture, salt was more than seasoning; it symbolized permanence. Just as salt preserves food from decay, YeHoVaH's covenant never spoils or loses its strength. His promises are eternal and unshakable. For this reason, many families dip bread in salt as a declaration, "We remember that Your covenant is everlasting." Yet it is important to understand that this tradition is not commanded. Some families choose to dip the bread, others do not. Both are honorable expressions, for what matters most is the heart, giving thanks together, remembering YeHoVaH's faithfulness and declaring that His Word is life.*

Think of it this way, bread represents life and salt represents preservation. Together they remind us of that YeHoVaH's Word gives life and His covenant endures forever.]

Leader
On the night He was betrayed, Yeshua took bread, gave thanks and broke it, saying, *"This is My body which is given for you; do this in remembrance of Me"* (**Luke 22:19** AMP). As we eat this bread together, we remember His sacrifice, His suffering and the abundant life He has imparted to us. This bread is more than a symbol; it is a declaration that His body was broken for our healing and through His death we have received eternal life.

Yeshua answered, *"I am the bread which is life! Whoever comes to me will never go hungry, and whoever trust in me will never be thirsty"* (**John 6:35** CJB).

As we partake of this bread on Shabbat, we proclaim that He sustains our lives alone and we honor the eternal covenant sealed through His body.

Together: Everyone Reads

Hebrew Translation
Ba-ruch at-tah YeHoVaH,
E-lo-hei-nu me-lekh ha-o-lam
ha-mo-tzi Yeshua ha-le-chem ha-chai
min ha-E'retz.

English Translation
Blessed are you, YeHoVaH, our God, King of the Universe, who brings forth Yeshua, The Living Bread from the earth. Amen

16. Kiddish-Blessing Over the Wine (or Grape Juice)
*[The Kiddush is more than a blessing; it is the sanctification of Shabbat itself. A special cup of wine or grape juice is lifted as a divine declaration, setting this day apart unto YeHoVaH. The word Kiddush means "sanctification," and through it we proclaim that this day is set apart, filled with joy, covenant and thanksgiving. Wine is a symbol of gladness, as it is written: "Wine that makes glad the heart of man" (**Psalm 104:15**). On Shabbat, we rejoice in the presence of Avinu, our Father, celebrating His goodness, His faithfulness and the rest He has given us from the beginning of creation. Lifting our cups together, we declare that our joy, strength and hope are found in Him alone. With grateful hearts we say the ancient words: **L'Chaim! - To Life!**]*

Leader
*"This cup is the New Covenant in my blood. Do this as often as you drink it, in remembrance of me" (**1 Corinthians 11:25** ESV).* As we drink the cup, we remember the precious blood of Messiah poured out for the forgiveness of sins and the sealing of an eternal covenant.

It is written: *Also he took a cup of wine, made the b´rakhah (blessing), and gave it to them, saying, "All of you, drink from it! For this is my blood, which ratifies the New Covenant, my blood shed on behalf of many, so that they may have their sins forgiven"* (**Matthew 26:27–28** CJB).

And again, He declared, *"This is My blood of the [new] covenant, [My blood] which is being poured out for many [for the forgiveness of sins]"* (**Mark 14:24** AMP).

As we partake, we proclaim that the blood of Yeshua has washed us, redeemed us and brought us near to the Father. Just as the prophet Isaiah wrote, *"… Though your sins are like scarlet, they shall be white as snow…"* (**Isaiah 1:18** ESV).

On this Shabbat, the cup reminds us that we are not only forgiven but also filled with joy, hope and life everlasting.

Together: Everyone Reads

Hebrew Translation
Ba-ruch at-tah YeHoVaH,
E-lo-hei-nu me-lekh ha-o-lam
bo-rci p'ri ha-ga-fen.

English Translation
Blessed are you, YeHoVaH, our God, King of the Universe, Creator of the fruit of the vine. Amen

Together: Everyone Reads

L'Chaim! To Life, in Yeshua the Messiah!

17. Proclaiming the Sanctity of Shabbat

[The leader and family or guest will take turns proclaiming scripture.]

Leader
"On the seventh day Elohim finished His work which He had made and He rested on the seventh day from all His work which He had made."

Family/Guests:
"Elohim blessed the seventh day and sanctified it because in it He rested from all His work which Elohim created and made."
(***Genesis 2:2-3***)

Leader:
"O come, let us sing unto YeHoVaH; let us make a joyful noise to the Rock of our salvation!"

Family/Guests:
"Let us come before His presence with thanksgiving and make a joyful noise unto Him with psalms."

Leader:
"For YeHoVaH is a great Elohim and a great King above all gods."

Family/Guests:
"O come, let us worship and bow down; let us kneel before YeHoVaH our Maker."
(***Psalm 95:1–3, 6***)

Together: Everyone Reads

Blessed are You, YeHoVaH our Elohim, who sanctifies the Sabbath and has given us rest in Yeshua the Messiah. Amen

Song: *Your choice of praise and worship*

18. Blessing Before the Meal (*Modeled after Yeshua*)
*[We bless before the meal following the example of Yeshua, who always give thanks before breaking bread and sharing. After the meal we bless because the Torah commands us to. When we are satisfied, we humble ourselves and remember that all fullness comes from YeHoVaH (**Deuteronomy 8:10**). To bless before and after is to walk in both the example of Messiah and the commandment of Scripture, keeping our hearts in gratitude and humility.]*

Together: Everyone Reads

Prayer
Blessed are You, YeHoVaH, our Elohim, King of the Universe, who brings forth bread from the earth. Thank You for this food set before us, for the work of our hands and for Your faithfulness that never fails. As Yeshua gave thanks before breaking bread, so we give thanks now, acknowledging You as the Giver of all good things. May this meal be sanctified for strength, health and joy in Your presence. Amen

The meal is enjoyed with gladness and simplicity. Between courses or before the meal you can:

- *Read from Scripture (**Psalm 92, Isaiah 58 or Exodus 20**)*
- *Sing or play soft worship or traditional melodies*

19. Blessing After the Meal (*Commanded in Torah*)

Leader
It is written: *"When you have eaten and are satisfied, then you shall bless [YeHoVaH] the LORD, your [Elohim] God*

for the good land which He has given you" (***Deuteronomy 8:10*** AMP)."

Together: Everyone Reads

Prayer
Blessed are You, YeHoVaH our Elohim, King of the Universe, who has fed us, satisfied us and given us every good thing. Thank You for filling our bodies with strength and our hearts with joy. We acknowledge that every good gift comes from Your hand; we humble ourselves before You, giving You all glory and praise.

As it is written: *"The eyes of all look to You [in hopeful expectation], And You give them their food in due time. You open Your hand And satisfy the desire of every living thing"* (***Psalm 145:15–16*** AMP). Truly, Your mercy endures forever.

Blessed are You, YeHoVaH our Elohim, who nourishes the entire world in goodness, with grace, kindness and compassion. You give bread to all flesh and through Your great goodness we have never lacked, nor will we lack food forever, for the sake of Your great Name. For You are YeHoVaH, who nourishes and sustains all, who does good to all and who provides food for every creature which You have created. Blessed are You, YeHoVaH, who nourishes all. Amen

20. Messiah at the Center

Leader
Remember, every blessing, candle and loaf of bread points to Yeshua, the Light of the world, the Bread of Life and the True Vine.

Together: Everyone Reads

"Come to Me, all who are weary and heavily burdened [religious rituals that provide no peace], and I will give you rest [refreshing your souls with salvation]" (**Matthew 11:28** AMP). Shabbat is not about what we must do. It is about receiving what He has already done.

Shabbat Shalom!

Reader Review: *A Beautiful Revelation of Yehovah's Rest. "At 90 years old, I've walked through many seasons of faith.* **The Gift of Shabbat** *has touched my heart like few things ever have. Through its pages, I discovered that Shabbat is not just a day of rest but a divine invitation from Yehovah to stop, breathe and dwell in His presence. This book revealed the beauty of the true Sabbath and the Torah, helping me understand the joy and holiness of setting this time apart. Now, each week my family and I gather to honor Shabbat as we share laughter, peace and worship together. The Gift of Shabbat is written with grace, truth and revelation that speaks straight to the soul. It reminds us that Yehovah's commandments are not burdens but blessings. They are gifts meant to draw us closer to Him. My prayer is that everyone who reads this book will come to know this same peace, truth and salvation that only Yehovah can give." By: Betty, age 90 Mother, Grandmother, Great-Grandmother, Great-Great-Grandmother and Sabbath Keeper*

Chapter 7
The Flow of Shabbat: A Day of Worship, Rest and Renewal

"It is a good thing to give thanks unto [YeHoVaH] the LORD, and to sing praises unto thy name, O Most High: To shew forth thy lovingkindness in the morning, and thy faithfulness every night" (**Psalm 92:1–2** KJV).

The Rhythm of Shabbat

Shabbat morning does not begin with hurry but with peace. After the beauty of Friday evening, Saturday rises like the dawn, inviting us to worship, rest and delight in the covenant of our Father. From sunrise to sunset, Shabbat carries a divine rhythm, morning worship, afternoon renewal and evening reflection.

From ancient times, this rhythm has been anchored in worship and the reading of the Word. The traditions of Israel were to gather in the synagogue to read the Torah and proclaim what the prophets prophesied. Yeshua embraced this rhythm of worship when He read from the scroll of Isaiah in the synagogue (***Luke 4:16-21***). Today, as followers of Messiah, we embrace the fullness of Scripture, Torah, Prophets and the New Covenant writings. Together they reveal YeHoVaH's covenant and the testimony of Yeshua.

For some, Shabbat worship takes place in assemblies, congregations or churches on Saturday mornings. Others begin with family worship on Friday evening and join with the wider community the next day. Some choose to honor the rhythm of service within their homes, creating a home church setting where family and friends join in study and prayer. However it is observed, Shabbat morning sets the tone for the day to open the Scriptures, lift our hearts in worship and align our lives with the Kingdom that is coming.

Shabbat Morning: Worship and the Word

We begin unrushed. Sometimes we sleep a little longer; sometimes we rise early with joy. Either way, we enter the morning with peace. A breakfast already prepared sets the tone as we gather around the table. After eating, we may go for a morning walk or ride, enjoying the beauty of creation, the trees, sky and songs of the birds all bearing witness to the handiwork of our Father.

When we return, we open our Bibles and bring out our study materials. With the children, we enjoy Bible drills, helping them write the Word on their hearts. Together we read the weekly Torah portion (*The 52-week cycle is listed in chapter 15*). From there, we move into a time of Torah worship, studying the Word deeply and allowing it to come alive by the Spirit.

A Flow for Morning Worship

1. Opening Blessing and Prayer
Thank You Father, for the gift of life and the breath in our lungs. Thank You for placing our feet on the floor this morning, giving us strength to rise and blessing us with another day to see each other again. We set this time apart to glorify You, rest in Your goodness and receive the life of Your Word. Amen

2. Songs of Praise
Music sets the tone for intimacy and joy. You may choose

your own worship songs that will reflect God's faithfulness, the beauty of rest and the Kingship of Yeshua.

3. Recommended Psalms

- Psalm 92 (*A Song for the Sabbath Day*)
- Psalm 19 (*The Law of YeHoVaH is Perfect*)
- Psalm 100 (*Enter His Gates with Thanksgiving*)

4. Reading the Word

- Torah
- Prophets (*Haftarah*)
- New Covenant (*Brit Hadashah*)

Blessing Before the Torah Reading

Together: Everyone Reads

Hebrew Translation
Ba-ruch at-tah YeHoVaH,
E-lo-hei-nu me-lekh ha-o-lam,
asher ba-char ba-nu mi-kol ha-amim,
v'natan la-nu et Torato.
Ba-ruch at-tah YeHoVaH,
noten ha-Torah.

English Translation
Blessed are You, YeHoVaH our God, King of the Universe, who has chosen us from among all peoples and given us His Torah. Blessed are You, YeHoVaH, Giver of the Torah.

5. Devotion & Discussion
Share insights, ask questions, encourage children and guests to take part.

6. Prayer & Intercession
Pray for your home, community, Israel and the nations. Invite Ruach HaKodesh (*Set Apart Spirit, The Holy Spirit*) to guide your prayers.

Shabbat Afternoon: Rest and Renewal

"…In returning and rest you shall be saved; in quietness and in trust shall be your strength" (***Isaiah 30:15*** ESV).

After the Word, we share lunch together as a family. The afternoon becomes a time of renewal. Some may choose to rest, nap or simply sit in stillness. Others may want to play outside, go for a swim, play games and enjoy the children YeHoVaH has blessed us with. These moments are not wasted; they are gifts of connection, laughter and joy.

Gift of Stillness

Psalm 46:10 ESV says: *"Be still and know that I am God."* The Hebrew word *raphah* means "to release or let go". You may want to do the following:

- Sit in silence and listen for His voice
- Walk in creation and reflect on His works
- Journal
- Read Scripture or meditate on a passage
- Rest your body and renew your spirit

Yeshua Himself withdrew to quiet places to pray (***Luke 5:16***). His rhythm of retreat becomes our example of rest. It is not laziness, it is alignment.

Study and Family Reflection

Afternoons are also perfect for deeper study or conversation. Read a devotional, listen to a teaching or revisit the Torah portion. As a family, take time to share what stood out during worship, ask how you can pray for one another and bless each other in His name. This is how faith is passed down from generation to the next generation.

Shabbat Evening: Anticipation and Gratitude

As the sun lowers, Shabbat enters its final hours. This is not yet Havdalah, it is still Shabbat. The evening is marked by quietness, joy, thanksgiving and reflection. Your evening may look like the following:

- Sharing a light meal together
- Singing songs of gratitude
- Reflecting on how YeHoVaH has spoken to you personally during the day
- Praying as a family
- Giving thanks for rest and renewal

Shabbat closes as it began with worship and blessing. From Friday sunset to Saturday sunset, it is a journey of His presence, a rehearsal for the eternal rest that awaits us in Yeshua the Messiah. Shabbat is His gift to you, but adoration is your gift to Him.

Reflection Questions

1. How can you make Shabbat morning both joyful and focused on the Word?
2. What does true rest look like for your soul in the afternoon?
3. What is one area of your life that needs His healing, if you would simply slow down and let Him speak?

Declaration

This is the day YeHoVaH has made; I will rejoice and be glad in it (***Psalm 118:24***). I receive the stillness of Shabbat as a gift from my Father. I accept deliverance from strife, stress and fear. I rest in His arms and listen for His voice. I am renewed, refreshed and restored in His presence. Amen

Reader Review: *"Reading **The Gift of Shabbat** really made us stop and think about the choices we make every day. We realized how easy it is to chase after things that don't last — success, comfort, the next big thing — but this book reminded us of Yehovah's promise of real rest and eternal peace. It's like coming to a fork in the road and finally seeing which path leads to life. Since we've started keeping Shabbat, we've felt more grounded, more at peace and closer to Yehovah than ever before. This book didn't just teach us about a day of rest; it helped us rediscover purpose in every breath." By: Brad and Loredana. Veteran and Business Owners.*

Chapter 8
Havdalah: Carrying the Light into the Week

"Behold, God is my salvation; I will trust, and will not be afraid..." (**Isaiah 12:2** ESV).

As the sun dips below the horizon and the final glow of Shabbat begins to fade, we come to one of the most beautiful and bittersweet moments of the entire Sabbath, Havdalah.

Havdalah (*separation*) is the ceremony that marks the end of Shabbat and the beginning of the new week. This moment is far more than a simple ritual; it is a prophetic transition. It reminds us that we carry the light of Shabbat into the darkness of the world. Is it possible that the Father begins days with evenings and brings the light into the darkness? Who is the light? Yeshua and through Him abiding in us we share the light (*Torah*) with the nations around the world.

It is not a biblical command but a beautiful custom that helps many families honor the transition from Shabbat back into the week. Whether you observe Havdalah with its traditional elements or simply close Shabbat with prayer and thanksgiving, the purpose is the same. It is to honor YeHoVaH by recognizing the holiness of His appointed time.

Why Havdalah Matters

In *Exodus 20*, God sanctifies the seventh day and separates it from the other six. Havdalah honors this distinction. As Shabbat ends, we do not simply *"go back to normal"*, we cross over into the week refreshed, realigned and carrying peace, purpose and light.

The goal is not to grieve Shabbat's departure but to take it with you into your work, your family and your calling.

"God saw the light was good (pleasing, useful) and He affirmed and sustained it; and God separated the light [distinguishing it] from the darkness" (**Genesis 1:4** AMP).

Havdalah is a reenactment of this divine separation, a line drawn in time that sets you apart. The following is a Havdalah guide that we use as a family for each Sabbath closing. Again, this is just an example. You and your family may want to close out your Sabbath a separate way or even add your own family preferences.

Havdalah Service Guide

1. Items Needed
- Candle holder
- Wine or grape juice
- Tiny glasses
- Saucer (holds the cup for overflowing)
- Aromatic spices (cinnamon, cloves, etc.)
- Head coverings ***optional***

2. Blessing Over the Wine
[Havdalah is the same as the one we recite when welcoming the Sabbath, the HaGafen (The Wine or Grape Juice) blessing. The cup is traditionally filled to the brim and even allowed to overflow slightly onto the saucer. This overflow is a meaningful symbol, standing for the abundance of blessings that flow from Shabbat into the week ahead. The blessing is spoken before drinking but the wine itself is not consumed until the Havdalah ceremony is complete, marking a respectful close for this set apart day.]

Leader

Havdalah reminds us of the joy and sanctity connected to both the beginning and the end of Shabbat. It also stands for the overflow of blessings from Shabbat into our new approaching week.

Hebrew Transliteration
Ba-ruch at-tah YeHoVaH,
E-lo-hei-nu me-lech ha-o-lam,
bo-rei p'ri ha-ga-fen.

English Transliteration
Blessed are You, YeHoVaH, our God, King of the Universe, Creator of the fruit of the vine. Amen

3. Blessing Over the Spices

[During the Havdalah service, we smell fragrant spices as a gentle reminder of the blessings we have experienced throughout the Sabbath. Common spices include cloves and cinnamon, though others like hyssop and anise may also be used. A special blessing is then recited over the spices.]

Leader

These sweet aromas help uplift our spirits as Shabbat leaves, symbolizing the beauty and peace it brings. This fragrance serves to stir our senses and preserve the sweetness of Shabbat a little longer. Even as Shabbat departs, its sweetness remains, pointing us back to the eternal rest promised in Yeshua.

Hebrew Transliteration
Ba-ruch at-tah YeHoVaH,
E-lo-hei-nu me-lech ha-olam,
bo-rei mee-nei ve-sah-meem.

English Transliteration

Blessed are You, YeHoVaH, our God, King of the Universe, Creator of different types of spices. Amen

4. Blessing Over the Fire (*Light of the Flame*)

*[As we light the Havdalah candle, we are reminded that light was the very first thing created by YeHoVaH. This moment marks the close of the Sabbath and the beginning of a new week. For many, this act of lighting the candle is their first intentional action of the new week since lighting fires is traditionally refrained from during the Sabbath according to **Exodus 35:3** ESV, "You shall kindle no fire in all your dwelling places on the Sabbath day."]*

Leader

With this light, we honor the Creator and step forward with renewed purpose. The flame symbolizes the transition from rest to purpose as we move from the consecrated stillness of Shabbat into the work and creativity of the coming days.

Hebrew Transliteration

Ba-ruch at-tah YeHoVaH,
E-lo-hei-nu me-lech ha-olam,
bo-rei meh-or-ee ha-esh.

English Transliteration

Blessed are You, YeHoVaH, our God, King of the Universe, Creator of the light of the fire. Amen

5. The Blessing of Separation (*HaMavdil*)

Hebrew Transliteration

Ba-ruch at-tah YeHoVaH, E-lo-hei-nu me-lech ha-olam, ha-mahv-dil ben ko-deshleh-chol, ben or leh-cho-shech, ben Yis-ra-el la-a-mim, ben yom ha-sh'vee-ee le-she-shet ye-mei ha-ma-a-seh. Ba-ruch at-tah YeHoVaH, ha-mahv-dil ben ko-desh leh-chol.

English Transliteration
Blessed are You, YeHoVaH, our God, King of the Universe, who distinguishes between the holy and the profane, light and darkness, between Israel and the nations, between the seventh day and the six days of work. Blessed are You, YeHoVaH, who separates between the holy and the profane. Amen

6. The End of Shabbat
After all the blessings
- Drink the wine or grape juice
- Extinguish the candle in the overflowed wine or grape juice
- Say to one another

"Shavua Tov" - Have a good week!

Reader Review: *"I absolutely love Shabbat. It's the true day of rest, set apart by Yehovah as a time to pause, refresh and realign our hearts with Him. There's something so amazing about entering into that divine rest. People may try to hide this truth. However, they can never block what Yehovah has ordained. Observing His Feasts and honoring His appointed times has brought such peace and joy into my life. I'm deeply thankful for this book because it reveals these powerful truths and carries the potential to transform lives." By: Samuel, Student and Sabbath Keeper*

Chapter 9
The Book of Remembrance: When Covenant Is Recorded in Heaven

"Then those who feared [YeHoVaH] the LORD spoke with one another. [YeHoVaH] the LORD paid attention and heard them, and a book of remembrance was written before him of those who feared [YeHoVaH] the LORD and esteemed his name" (***Malachi 3:16*** ESV).

The Heavenly Records

There are many books in heaven. The Scriptures speak of the Book of Life, the Book of Deeds and mysteriously the *Book of Remembrance*. This is not a metaphor. It is a record kept before YeHoVaH, written for those who fear Him, who speak of Him and who meditate on His name.

But what if this "remembrance" is directly tied to the one commandment that begins with the word *Remember*?

The Only Commandment That Begins With "Remember"

"Remember the Sabbath day, to keep it holy" (***Exodus 20:8*** ESV).

Out of the Ten Commandments, only one begins with "Remember." The Sabbath is the covenant seal between the Creator and His people and He knew it would be the one most easily forgotten or ignored.

The Sabbath is not just a tradition. It is a covenant marker. It is like an engagement ring between the Bridegroom and the Bride. When we honor the Sabbath, we proclaim:

- I know who made me.
- I know to whom I belong.

When we remember Him, He remembers us.

Lawlessness or Torah

Yeshua's warning in *Matthew 7:23* ESV is chilling:

"And then will I declare to them, "I never knew you; depart from Me, you workers of lawlessness."

The Greek word here for "lawlessness" is *anomia* meaning "without Torah." This is critical. Over time, when the Scriptures were translated, the Hebrew word Torah (*meaning instruction, covenant teaching, the light YeHoVaH gave His people*) was flattened into the Greek word *nomos* "law."

To modern ears, "law" sounds like legalism, rules or something we are freed from. However, Torah is YeHoVaH's covenant design, His loving instruction for how to live as His set-apart people.

So, when Yeshua said, *"Depart from Me, you workers of lawlessness,"* He was not rejecting people for lacking Roman law or man's law. He was saying:

"You rejected My Torah. You wanted forgiveness but not obedience. You wanted blessings but not My covenant."

Forgiveness Without Repentance

Today, many want to call on Yeshua for forgiveness but refuse to walk in His Words. They want the covering of His blood without the turning of their hearts. They only want His promises, never His commandments, just Fire Insurance.

Repentance is not simply saying, "I apologize, please forgive me." Repentance (*Teshuvah*) means to return or to turn away from sin and return home to YeHoVaH. The Torah is His covenant way of life. Just like the prodigal son: "*I will arise and go to my father…*" (**Luke 15:18-20** KJV).

Rejecting the Sabbath and His commands is to say, I choose my own pleasures over the joy of Your presence. I desire Your mercy but I refuse the terms of Your covenant. However, honoring the Sabbath is to declare Your presence above every earthly pleasure. I embrace not only Your mercy but also the beauty of Your covenant. Yeshua strongly warns that forgiveness without repentance is empty. Grace is never a license to sin; it is the power to walk in obedience and live in covenant with YeHoVaH.

The Book of Remembrance

Every act of covenant faithfulness is recorded. It is not wasted when you light the candles before sunset, honor His day and refuse distraction in order to sit at His feet. Heaven sees every time you remembered YeHoVaH, every moment you turned from distraction to seek His face, each meal you set apart, every song you lifted in praise and every choice you made to rest instead of rushing.

"I RECORDED IT," says YeHoVaH.

We cry, *"YeHoVaH, do You see me?"*
And the Book of Remembrance answers:
"Yes! I wrote it down!"

He Remembers His Covenant

"He remembers His covenant forever, the word that He commanded, for a thousand generations" (**Psalm 105:8** ESV).

You were created for covenant. The Sabbath is not optional; it is the sign that you belong to Him. It is the Bride's declaration: *"I am His and He is mine."*

One day, when the books are opened, He will say to those who honored His covenant:
"You remembered Me. I remember you."

For those who wanted His forgiveness without His Torah, who asked for His blessings but not His Words, He will say:
"Depart from Me. You chose lawlessness."

Reflection Question

The Sabbath is an essential part of the Torah, which means "instruction." Rejecting the Torah is rejecting YeHoVaH's divine order and living in lawlessness. What is your choice?

Reader Review: *"There is so much to learn in* **The Gift of Shabbat***. It has truly been an eye-opener for me. This book helped me see things I never noticed before and it deepened my understanding of Yehovah's rest in a powerful way. I would highly recommend this book to anyone who is willing to take a chance and read it. There's a wealth of knowledge and wisdom waiting inside."* By: Elisa, Nurse and VP

Chapter 10
The Secret Place: Dwelling in the Shadow of the Almighty

"He that dwelleth in the secret place of the most High shall abide under the shadow of the Almighty" (**Psalm 91:1** KJV).

Shabbat Is the Secret Place

Shabbat has never been about heavy rules. It has always been about a divine relationship, a day that reminds us of who He is and to whom we belong. It is the pause that reconnects us with eternity. It is not just a command; it is a covenant. Not just a law, it is love.

The world spins faster and louder each day with deadlines, events, screens or noise. Every seven days, the King of glory calls His children to:

- stop
- step away from the rush
- enter His garden again
- light the candles
- break the bread
- be still and know

The secret place is not a temple built by hands. It is not far away. It is a sacred moment in time, a meeting place where we encounter His presence. Shabbat is that secret place, a doorway into divine rest. In the stillness of Shabbat, heaven leans low; YeHoVaH's whisper fills the heart with peace. ***"I am here. I remember you. Come and remember Me."***

The Rhythm of Creation

From the very beginning, YeHoVaH set His rhythm in motion: *"And the evening and the morning were the first day"* (**Genesis 1:5** KJV). *"And the evening and the morning were the second day"* (**Genesis 1:8** KJV).

In His calendar, a new day begins at sunset not at midnight, from darkness into light, from labor into rest. So it is with Shabbat, it begins Friday at sunset and ends Saturday at sunset. A circle of time, written into creation itself, reminding us of His covenant heartbeat.

Why the Seventh Day Matters

When looking at a calendar, you will notice that the first day of the week is Sunday and the seventh day is Saturday. From the very beginning of creation, YeHoVaH established the rhythm of time. The Torah declares each day begins in darkness and moves into light. Since the fourth day of creation, each day is measured from sunset to sunset. Therefore, the true Sabbath begins on Friday at sunset and concludes on Saturday at sunset, just as the Father ordained from the foundation of the world.

How can we allow ourselves to be deceived when the truth is written plainly before our eyes? The traditions of men for generations have taught that Sunday is the Sabbath, rewriting what YeHoVaH established at creation. The Scriptures are the absolute truth, not a lie. Sunday is the first day of the week, not the seventh. *"Now upon the first day of the week, very early in the morning, they came unto the sepulcher..."* (**Luke 24:1** KJV). Yeshua rose on the first day; the seventh day, however, had already been set apart at creation. He rested, blessed it and made it holy. Sabbath is not man's idea; it is Father's commandment.

Deception in the Pulpit

In many denominations you will never be allowed to preach in their pulpits and houses of worship unless you have been ordained by them. I have been told, *"You must preach Baptist doctrine."* We must ask, whose doctrine are we preaching, man's or YeHoVaH's? They can hang the Commandments on church walls yet never keep them. What good is it if you are being deceived by man's replacement theology rather than what the actual Word says? Read it for yourself: *"Remember the Sabbath day, to keep it holy"* (***Exodus 20:8*** KJV). When man redefines what YeHoVaH has already defined, deception will follow.

The Trap of Religion

Could it be that many have been conditioned to follow religious traditions instead of the living Word of YeHoVaH? They are taught exactly what to say, what they may do and what they must avoid. These man-made rules hold people accountable to systems of control rather than to the Scriptures themselves.

It reminds me of how leaders once sat in the seat of Moses, twisting authority to serve their own agendas while denying the true Word of YeHoVaH: *"Do this, don't do that; you may not go there, you cannot say that."* Yet in all their commands, they silenced the truth: *"Be ye holy, for I am holy"* (***1 Peter 1:16*** KJV).

Religion builds walls and breeds pride; holiness calls us back to the heart of YeHoVaH. The danger is the longer we live, the deeper the roots of dead religion can entangle our hearts. Religion without truth will never lead to life; it can only lead a soul to a devil's hell.

The Deception of Tradition

Why is this confusion so widespread? What you are taught, you begin to believe; what you believe, you begin to defend, even when it is not the truth. The enemy knows this. He has worked to fill schools and seminaries with doctrines that perpetuate tradition over Scripture. For generations, instructors have repeated teachings that do not align with the Hebrew foundations of the faith. Many leaders, without returning to the Word, have unknowingly led the people astray. One of the enemy's most effective tactics is to use the very classrooms where shepherds are trained to plant mixture, so the flock inherits deception rather than truth.

The Call to Truth

The absolute truth does not come from a classroom or a denomination; it comes from the Scriptures themselves. At the Great White Throne Judgment, you will not be judged by what your instructor or pastor said. You will be accountable for what YeHoVaH has spoken in His Word. His Word warns us: *"Be hot or cold, but if you are lukewarm, you will be rejected"*(***Revelation 3:16***). Mixture is not devotion and compromise is not obedience. Think carefully, could it be that the enemy has convinced us we are honoring the Father while we are, in reality, denying His Word?

The Stewardship of Your Voice

If you are in a congregation where tradition is preached above Scripture, open your eyes. When you give your tithes and offerings, your money becomes a voice. If it supports lies, you are empowering deception. Let your giving cry out for truth. Tell your leaders your concerns. They may not even know the truth themselves. The Church must preach the Word as it is written and if they refuse, withhold your support. If they persist in falsehood, remove yourself. Find a place to worship where the Word is honored, the truth is proclaimed plainly, so you can read it, see it and live it for yourself.

An Invitation, Not Just Information

This journey has not only been about facts; it has been about an invitation also. Shabbat is not merely something to know but something to enter. It is not only knowledge; it is a relationship.

You have not just read about Shabbat; you have been invited:

- To join the rhythm of heaven
- Walk in step with the King
- Become the bride who is not late
- Not to be distracted
- Not to be busy with lesser things

From Shabbat to the Feasts

Shabbat is the beginning, not the end. It is the doorway into something greater. For YeHoVaH has more appointments, consecrated rehearsals called *Mo'edim*, the Feast Days:

- Passover
- Unleavened Bread
- First fruits
- Shavuot
- Yom Teruah
- Yom Kippurim
- Sukkot

Each feast is a divine rehearsal that reveals Yeshua and draws the Bride closer to the Bridegroom. *"These are the feasts of [YeHoVaH] the LORD, even holy convocations, which ye shall proclaim in their [moedim] seasons"* (***Leviticus 23:4*** KJV).

In Hebrew, the word for YeHoVaH's appointed times is moedim. It comes from the root *moed*, meaning an appointed time, season or meeting. These are not man-made holidays but divine appointments set by YeHoVaH Himself. The moedim are the rhythm of Heaven written into the calendar of the earth. They are YeHoVaH's feasts, not Israel's feasts or Jewish feasts but YeHoVaH's appointed times. Each moed is a rehearsal, a prophetic picture of redemption through the Messiah and an invitation for His people to meet with Him.

The Sabbath along with the Feasts teach us to rehearse. Together, they form the calendar of heaven, blueprint of redemption and the map from the Garden to eternity.

Reader Review: *"This book is truly amazing! The revelation within* **The Gift of Shabbat** *is powerful and life-changing. It presents an appeal for every believer to turn away from the traditions of men and lay down every excuse that keeps them from the truth. This book challenged and inspired me to align my life with the Word of GOD. It's exactly what this generation needs to hear, not the voice of a wolf in sheep's clothing." By: Eddie, CEO*

Chapter 11
The Cost of Covenant: Death for Life

The Great Exchange

"Some trade life now for death later, while others are willing to die now to themselves to have life eternally."– Cumbee's

Hear me, this is the great exchange of eternity. The world whispers, *"Protect your life, cling to your comfort, secure yourself now,"* but Yeshua declared with thunder: *"Everyone who wishes to save his life-it will be lost for my sake. He who loses his life in this world for my sake-will save his soul for the life of the world to come"* (**Matthew 16:25** HTV).

Dear reader, pause and reflect on this truth. It is not merely a suggestion but a divine command. Whoever seeks to cling to their own life will lose it; yet whoever surrenders their life will truly find it.

The world has deceived the church in many ways. Its message is the opposite of the Kingdom's call. The world whispers, choose life now even if it leads to death later; live for the moment, enjoy pleasure while you can, compromise today and worry about eternity tomorrow. These promises are empty; they exchange eternal life for fleeting satisfaction.

YeHoVaH's Kingdom calls out to mankind with a different cry: *"He that loveth his life shall lose it; and he that hateth his life in this world shall keep it unto life eternal"* (***John 12:25*** KJV). In exchange, you will inherit eternal life. The way of the Kingdom is not one of clinging to self but of surrendering all, that we may truly live. The choice is before us, life now for death later or death now for life eternal. I ask you, which one will you choose?

The Man at the Stake

Picture this scenario, an ordinary man of flesh and blood, a husband, father and son. His name erased from history's records but engraved in heaven's scrolls.

Word spread in his village and surrounding towns, *"If you keep this Sabbath day holy, you will die."* Knowing the warning had been issued, he still did not wavier. Soldiers marched into his house on Friday after sunset. An aggressive officer gave him one more chance to deny and just compromise his faith to escape the flames that awaited him.

Instead, he lifted his eyes, unshaken and said, "I am already burning within me. Bring the people, bring the crowds, for I must tell them what is worth living for if we are all destined to die in the end. Do you think these ropes bind me? No, my faith binds me stronger than any rope or chain. My life is nothing without the One who gave it."

Then he cried out the name of YeHoVaH, *"For the which cause I also suffer these things: nevertheless I am not ashamed: for I know whom I have believed, and am persuaded that he is able to keep that which I have committed unto him against that day"* (***2 Timothy 1:12*** KJV).

They tied him to the stake as the wood was being piled high around him. The crowd mocked him. Mothers shielded their children's eyes while fathers clenched their fists in hatred toward him. As he lifted his head, his words rang out as thunder.

My Yeshua is the fire! For my GOD is a consuming fire (***Hebrews 12:29***)! He showed up for the three Hebrew children. My choice is to glorify Him today. If He allows this fire to consume my flesh, then let my ashes be a testimony. If He delivers me, I will still be a living testimony. For you can only destroy this body but my Father alone can destroy both soul and body in hell!

"And fear not them which kill the body, but are not able to kill the soul: but rather fear him which is able to destroy both soul and body in hell" (***Matthew 10:28*** KJV).

The flames licked his feet as his face shone like Stephen's.

"But he, full of the Ruach HaKodesh (Set Apart Spirit, The Holy Spirit), looked up to heaven and saw God's Sh'khinah (glory), with Yeshua standing at the right hand of God. Look! He exclaimed, I see heaven opened and the Son of Man standing at the right hand of God" (***Acts 7:55-56*** CJB)!

His last cry pierced the stony hearts of the crowd, **"Repent! Return to YeHoVaH! Stand and become children of the Highest!"** As the smoke rose, so did his testimony. Will you stand like this man or will you compromise?

The Cost of Our Forefathers

This man was not alone. He was one of thousands who sealed their testimony with their own blood.

"And they overcame him by the blood of the Lamb, and by the word of their testimony; and they loved not their lives unto the death" (***Revelation 12:11*** KJV).

When Rome exalted Sunday above Sabbath, those who clung to the seventh day were branded heretics. They lost land, families and some were murdered for their Faith.

"For ye had compassion of me in my bonds, and took joyfully the spoiling of your goods, knowing in yourselves that ye have in heaven a better and an enduring substance" (**Hebrews 10:34** KJV).

The Waldensians fled into mountains, whispering Torah in caves. Parents instructed their children, *"Remember the sabbath day, to keep it holy"*(**Exodus 20:8** KJV).

"Six days shalt thou labour, and do all thy work: But the seventh day is the sabbath of [YeHoVaH] the LORD thy God: in it thou shalt not do any work… For in six days [YeHoVaH] the LORD made heaven and earth, the sea, and all that in them is, and rested the seventh day: wherefore [YeHoVaH] the LORD blessed the sabbath day, and hallowed [set apart] it" (**Exodus 20:9-11** KJV).

They knew if they were discovered, it meant death, yet they stood firm in YeHoVaH's covenant.

During the Inquisitions, men and women stood accused, *"Do you keep the Sabbath?"* Confessing yes, meant death. Compromising was denying their faith. However, many chose death and their voices echoed like the apostles.

"Then Peter and the other apostles answered and said, We ought to obey God rather than men" (**Acts 5:29** KJV).

Their ashes became sermons and their blood cried louder than the words from the modern-day watered down pulpits.

"And what shall I more say? for the time would fail me to tell of Gideon, and of Barak, and of Samson, and of Jephthae; of David also, and Samuel, and of the prophets: Who through faith subdued kingdoms, wrought righteousness, obtained promises, stopped the mouths of lions… They were stoned, they were sawn asunder, were tempted, were slain with the sword: they wandered about in sheepskins and goatskins; being destitute, afflicted, tormented; (Of whom the world was not worthy:) they wandered in deserts, and in mountains, and in dens and caves of the earth" (**Hebrews 11:32–38** KJV).

What is Your Price

Ask yourself plainly, what is your price? Will you trade your soul for comfort, reputation or a momentary gain? The world pays in gold, silver, money and cheap applause. These may include thirty pieces of silver, thirty dollars, thirty thousand, a million; any price short of your life is a price at which you can be bought. If you can be bought, you are not free.

Consider how easily a heart can be sold, a compromise for favor, concession for gain and silence for safety. These purchases come in many forms such as a job, lifestyle or an image. They are all bargains that cost less than everything but cost everything in the end. History remembers Judas Iscariot, eternity remembers us.

The Kingdom calls for a different currency, your life. Following Yeshua is to be willing to lose your life in this age so you will be saved in the age to come. It is to say, with every fiber of your being, "Not my will, but Yours." This is not sentimental language; it is the required cost. We do not pay with money, status or convenience; instead, we pay with surrender.

So now I ask you, are you willing to pay that cost? If your answer is anything less than everything, then something or someone still owns you. If your answer is yes, then live as one surrendered; walk in obedience, embrace humility and stand ready for whatever may come. There is coming a day when we will all stand before the Judge.

Will you be bought for less or will you be sold out for the Kingdom?

A Word to This Generation

YeHoVaH has chosen you to live at this specific time to affect your generation with the absolute truth. How is this possible? You must use your voice and stand on YeHoVaH's Word. It is His instructions to follow and proclaim. Some will never truly live because they have never truly died; to their self, warfare, ways or will. I challenge you even as Paul was teaching to the Galatians:

"I am crucified with [Yeshua] Christ: nevertheless I live; yet not I, but [Yeshua] Christ liveth in me: and the life which I now live in the flesh I live by the faith of the Son of God, who loved me, and gave himself for me" (**Galatians 2:20** KJV).

We are drowning in entertainment, tradition and distraction. Yeshua said: *"And ye shall know the truth, and the truth shall make you free"* (**John 8:32** KJV).

So, I ask you, will you be the one who brings the fire into your church, community and family? Will you stand and proclaim YeHoVaH's Word no matter the cost?

"Thus saith [YeHoVaH] the LORD, Stand ye in the ways, and see, and ask for the old paths, where is the good way,

and walk therein, and ye shall find rest for your souls. But they said, We will not walk therein" (***Jeremiah 6:16*** KJV).

YeHoVaH's only begotten Son shed His precious blood for you and me. Yeshua freely gave His life and YeHoVaH raised Him from the dead. Will you be bound by men and their tradition or be free in Yeshua the Messiah?

"Ye are bought with a price; be not ye the servants of men" (***1 Corinthians 7:23*** KJV).

Precious soul, please hear the warning. I ask you, what will you do with this truth today? Time is fading and it will soon be gone. Do not be unprepared to meet the judgement.

A Call to Men, Women and Children (*Sons and Daughters*)

"And if it seem evil unto you to serve [YeHoVaH] the LORD, choose you this day whom ye will serve… but as for me and my house, we will serve [YeHoVaH] the LORD" (***Joshua 24:15*** KJV).

Men of Valor:
"Fight the good fight of faith, lay hold on eternal life, whereunto thou art also called, and hast professed a good profession before many witnesses" (***1 Timothy 6:12*** KJV).

The Decree of the Man of Valor
(Prepared for the Sons of the King - If you would like this powerful decree, you can visit our website at Cumbees.com)

I stand this day before YeHoVaH, my King and my Savior. I come into this covenant with You to walk as a man of honor, strength and faith. I will not abandon my calling but will take full responsibility for my life, wife and children.

I will cover my house in prayer, guard it from the schemes of the enemy and establish it upon Your unshakable Word. I will love my wife as Yeshua loves His Bride, laying down my life and desires so that she may flourish in peace, strength and joy.

I will bless my children and declare their destiny. I will raise them to know You, hear Your voice, walk in Your ways and stand firm in a world that bows to idols. I will teach them to honor authority, live responsibly and carry the Kingdom wherever they go.

I will confront darkness, not retreat; I will pursue justice, not compromise. I will extend mercy and will not withhold my compassion. I will work with diligence to provide for my family's needs, knowing that provision flows first from the hand of YeHoVaH.

I will walk in forgiveness, extending grace to those who have hurt me; I will seek reconciliation where relationships have been broken. I will repent quickly, learn from my failures and walk uprightly, for I am a man under authority, accountable to the King of the Universe. I will honor Your name YeHoVaH in my home, be faithful, obey Your Word and carry out Your will in my life.

Father, I ask You for the wisdom, courage and strength to live out this decree every day of my life, not in my own strength but in the power of Your Ruach Kodesh. I proclaim You raised Yeshua from the dead; I fully trust in You.

"As for me and my house, we will serve YeHoVaH" (***Joshua 24:15***).

Women of Virtue:
"She openeth her mouth with wisdom; and in her tongue is the law of kindness" (***Proverbs 31:26*** KJV).

Decree of the Virtuous Woman
(Prepared for the Daughters of the King - If you would like this powerful decree, you can visit our website at Cumbees.com)

I stand this day before YeHoVaH, my King and my Savior. I come into this covenant with You to walk as Your beloved daughter, clothed in strength, dignity and wisdom.

YeHoVaH, I love you with all my heart, soul, mind and strength. I will follow Yeshua, my Bridegroom, wherever He leads.

I decree that my life will be a testimony of holiness, faith and love. I will not bow to the spirit of this age. I will walk in the beauty of holiness, carrying the fragrance of Yeshua every day.

YeHoVaH, I will honor and support my husband as unto You, strengthening him with prayer, encouragement and respect. I will stand beside him as a covenant partner, not shrinking back in fear but advancing with him in faith.

I will nurture my children in the fear of YeHoVaH, speaking life and blessing over them, training them to hear Your voice and guiding them into their Kingdom purpose.

I will guard the atmosphere of my home, filling it with peace, purity and praise. My words will build, not tear down; my hands will serve with joy, not resentment.

I will rise in courage when the enemy attacks, knowing I am a warrior bride, armed with Your Word and the fire of Ruach HaKodesh. I will forgive quickly, love deeply and live honorably, so that the generations after me will call me blessed.

I will walk in integrity, wisdom and discernment, using the gifts of Your Spirit entrusted to me for the glory of YeHoVaH.

Father, I ask You for the boldness and strength to live out this decree every day of my life, not in my own strength but in the power of Your Ruach Kodesh. I proclaim You raised Yeshua from the dead. I fully trust in You.

"As for me and my house, we will serve YeHoVaH" (***Joshua 24:15***).

Children of Obedience (Sons and Daughters):
"Children, obey your parents in [YeHoVaH] the Lord: for this is right. Honour thy father and mother; which is the first commandment with promise" (***Ephesians 6:1–2*** KJV).

The Decree of the Son
(Prepared for the Sons of the King - If you would like this powerful decree, you can visit our website at Cumbees.com)

I stand this day before YeHoVaH, my King and my Savior. I come into this covenant with You. I declare that I am Your son, chosen, forgiven and set apart for Your purpose.

Yeshua, my Redeemer and King I belong to You. My strength, worth and future are found in You alone.

I will honor my father and mother, learning from their instruction and walking in obedience, that I may grow in wisdom, strength and favor with YeHoVaH and man.

I will keep my heart pure and my mind clean, refusing the lies of the enemy and rejecting the snares of sin. I will guard my eyes, words and actions walking in holiness as a son of light.

I will choose courage over fear, truth over compromise and righteousness over rebellion. I will protect the weak, stand up for what is right and show kindness to others, reflecting the heart of You, my Heavenly Father.

I will train myself in Your Word and in prayer, that I may be strong in spirit and ready for every battle. I will prepare my life for the future, so that when the day comes, I may stand as a righteous man, faithful husband and loving father.

Father, I ask You for the boldness to live out this decree every day of my youth and manhood, not in my own strength but in the power of Your Ruach Kodesh. I proclaim You raised Yeshua from the dead. I fully trust in You.

"As for me and my house, we will serve YeHoVaH" (***Joshua 24:15***).

Decree of the Daughter
(Prepared for the Daughters of the King - If you would like this powerful decree, you can visit our website at Cumbees.com)

I stand this day before YeHoVaH, my King and my Savior. I come into this covenant with You. I declare that I am Your daughter, chosen, loved and set apart for Your glory.

Yeshua, my identity rests not in the world but in You. You are the One who created me, redeemed me and continues to call me by name.

I will honor my father and mother, walking in obedience and respect, so that I may grow in wisdom, favor and strength. I will keep my heart pure and my hands clean, refusing to follow the ways of darkness. I will not give my worth away cheaply, for I am a treasure in YeHoVaH's House.

I will speak truth, show kindness and walk humbly with You all the days of my life. I will guard my friendships and choose companions who love righteousness, so that I may be strengthened and not led astray.

I will learn to pray, hear the voice of my Shepherd and follow You with courage even when others turn away. I will honor my body as the temple of YeHoVaH, walking in holiness until the day I stand as a bride in covenant before You. I will not fear the future, for You have written my story and established my destiny.

Father, I ask You for the boldness to live out this decree every day of my youth and beyond, not in my own strength but in the power of Your Ruach Kodesh. I proclaim You raised Yeshua from the dead. I fully trust in You.

"As for me and my house, we will serve YeHoVaH" (***Joshua 24:15***).

Rise, repent, be restored and return to His presence, for YeHoVaH is calling His people back with power and refreshing.

"Repent ye therefore, and be converted, that your sins may be blotted out, when the times of refreshing shall come from the presence of [YeHoVaH] the Lord" (**Acts 3:19** KJV).

The Fire Still Burns

Do you remember the flames at the stakes, caves and the prisons? Their fire still burns.

"Upon this rock I will build my church; and the gates of hell shall not prevail against it" (**Matthew 16:18** KJV).

Even if only a faint ember stays, the breath of Ruach HaKodesh (*Set Apart Spirit, The Holy Spirit*) can stir it into a holy flame once more if you will yield and let Him.

"Quench not the Spirit" (**1Thessalonians 5:19** KJV).

They have stripped possessions, canceled voices and mocked faith but they cannot silence His truth.

"And they overcame him by the blood of the Lamb, and by the word of their testimony; and they loved not their lives unto the death" (**Revelation 12:11** KJV).

Like the Hebrew children, we declare:

"If it be so, our God whom we serve is able to deliver us from the burning fiery furnace, and he will deliver us out of thine hand, O king. But if not, be it known unto thee, O king, that we will not serve thy gods, nor worship the golden image which thou hast set up" (**Daniel 3:17-18** KJV).

Do you long for the Holy Fire you are reading about today? The fire of YeHoVaH is not like the flames of this world; it burns with a purity and power beyond anything known to man. He is no lukewarm spark. He is a Consuming Fire; every soul will one day stand before Him, tried and measured by His flame.

The Final Appeal

The hour of decision is upon you; the eternal choice between life and death, blessing and cursing, now stands before your soul.

"I call heaven and earth to record this day against you, that I have set before you life and death, blessing and cursing: therefore choose life, that both thou and thy seed may live" (**Deuteronomy 30:19** KJV).

"Some trade life now for death later, while others are willing to die now to themselves to have life eternally." – Cumbee's

"Knowing this, that our old man is crucified with him, that the body of sin might be destroyed, that henceforth we should not serve sin. For he that is dead is freed from sin. Now if we be dead with [Yeshua] Christ, we believe that we shall also live with him" (**Romans 6:6-8** KJV).

The call is clear; turn from your own ways and align your steps with His Holy Covenant.

"If thou turn away thy foot from the sabbath, from doing thy pleasure on my holy day; and call the sabbath a delight, the holy of [YeHoVaH] the LORD, honourable; and shalt honour him, not doing thine own ways, nor finding thine own pleasure, nor speaking thine own words: Then shalt thou delight thyself in [YeHoVaH] the LORD; and I will cause thee to ride upon the high places of the earth, and feed thee

with the heritage of Jacob thy father: for the mouth of [YeHoVaH] the LORD hath spoken it" (**Isaiah 58:13–14** KJV).

For the world passes but YeHoVaH's Word endures forever.

"The grass withereth, the flower fadeth: but the word of our God shall stand for ever" (**Isaiah 40:8** KJV).

"And the world passeth away, and the lust thereof: but he that doeth the will of God abideth for ever" (**1 John 2:17** KJV).

I will honor YeHoVaH's truth and His commandments; I will keep His Sabbath. With my life, I will testify that Yeshua is LORD, the Living Word that was made flesh.

"That at the name of [Yeshua] Jesus every knee should bow, of things in heaven, and things in earth, and things under the earth; And that every tongue should confess that [Yeshua the Messiah] Jesus Christ is Lord, to the glory of [Yehovah] God the Father" (**Philippians 2:10–11** KJV).

All will bow, all will confess, whether by faith now or by force at the Great White Throne Judgment. It's your decision.

Reader Review: *"What is revealed to us as we read the words on these pages and through the chapters of this, Life Spiritual Manual...Will enhance and transform every person to honor and serve YeHoVaH with a more determined committed heart. A renewed and magnificent relationship with Yeshua the King will likewise manifest as never before!" By: Robert, Minister*

Chapter 12
Shabbat Eternal: Rest, Warning and the Call to Covenant

"Thus saith [YeHoVaH] the LORD unto me; Go and stand in the gate of the children of the people, whereby the kings of Judah come in, and by the which they go out, and in all the gates of Jerusalem; And say unto them, Hear ye the word of [YeHoVaH] the LORD, ye kings of Judah, and all Judah, and all the inhabitants of Jerusalem, that enter in by these gates: Thus saith [YeHoVaH] the LORD; Take heed to yourselves, and bear no burden on the sabbath day, nor bring it in by the gates of Jerusalem; Neither carry forth a burden out of your houses on the sabbath day, neither do ye any work, but hallow ye the sabbath day, as I commanded your fathers. But they obeyed not, neither inclined their ear, but made their neck stiff, that they might not hear, nor receive instruction" (***Jeremiah 17:19–23*** KJV).

A Call at the Gates

The prophet Jeremiah was commanded to stand at the gates of Jerusalem and cry aloud, *"Sanctify the Sabbath day."* It was not a gentle suggestion. It was a divine command, carrying with its blessings for obedience and destruction for rebellion.

YeHoVaH promised if His people would honor the Sabbath, kings and princes would pass through Jerusalem's gates in glory and the city would endure forever. If they refused, the gates would burn with fire and judgment would fall. The choice then and the choice now is crystal clear, remember the Sabbath or face the penalty of forgetting.

Entering His Rest

The writer of Hebrews picks up this cry and presses it into eternity:

*"So there remains a Shabbat-keeping for God's people. For the one who has **entered** God's **rest** has also **rested from his** own **works**, as God did from his. Therefore, let us do our best to **enter** that **rest**; so that no one will fall short because of the same kind of disobedience"* (**Hebrews 4:9–11** CJB).

The Sabbath is not bondage; it is freedom. It is the sign that we trust YeHoVaH enough to lay down our striving and rest in His covenant. Refusing Shabbat is to live in unbelief, declaring that our ways are higher than His.

The Eternal Shabbat

Some say the Sabbath was only for Israel or only for the Old Covenant. Scripture testifies otherwise:

"For just as the new heavens and the new earth Which I will make will remain and Endure before Me, declares [YeHoVaH] the LORD, So shall your seed and your name remain. And it shall come to pass, that from one new moon to another, and from one sabbath to another, shall all flesh come to worship before Me, saith [YeHoVaH] the LORD" (***Isaiah 66:22–23*** AMP).

In the Millennial Reign of Messiah and in the New Heaven and the New Earth, the Sabbath will be kept by all flesh. Sabbath is not a relic of the past; it is a rhythm of eternity. It is heaven's heartbeat and those who belong to Yeshua the Messiah will walk in it forever.

The Penalty of Forgetting

The Scriptures do not soften the cost of disobedience:

- ***Exodus 31:14*** KJV *states, "Ye shall keep the sabbath therefore; for it is holy unto you: everyone that defileth it shall surely be put to death."*
- ***Ezekiel 20:12-13*** KJV *declares, "Moreover also I gave them my sabbaths, to be a sign between me and them… but the house of Israel rebelled… and my sabbaths they greatly polluted."*
- ***Isaiah 58:13-14*** KJV *warns, "If thou turn away thy foot from the sabbath, from doing thy pleasure on my holy day… then shalt thou delight thyself in [YeHoVaH] the LORD."*

Rejecting Shabbat is to reject covenant identity. Polluting it is to despise the Bridegroom's sign of love. Forgetting it is to risk hearing those dreadful words of Yeshua:

"And then I myself shall profess to them, I never knew you! Get away from me - All you workers of lawlessness" (***Matthew 7:23*** HTV)!

A Question for the Heart

So beloved, here is the question you may wrestle with:

Are you keeping Sabbath, the very day YeHoVaH sanctified at creation, commanded at Sinai, affirmed by the prophets, honored by Yeshua, practiced by the apostles and promised in eternity? If not, what excuse will you offer when you stand before Him?

This is not about earning salvation. It is about covenant love. Obedience is not legalism; it is love in action. Now that you know the truth, you are accountable for it. Mercy has revealed it to you and grace empowers you to walk in it. Yet the day of judgment will not overlook your choice; if you ignore it, you will be held accountable.

A Final Appeal

Our book was written with one cry in our hearts, that you would never have to hear Him say, **"Depart from Me, I never knew you."**

Today is the day to repent:

- Turn from the traditions of men
- Lay down your excuses
- Align your life with the rhythm of heaven
- Return back home to the Father, YeHoVaH

The Father is merciful and gracious with outstretched arms. His covenant still stands as well as the Sabbath that is set apart and consecrated from all other days. The Father's desire is that none should perish but all should enter into His eternal rest.

Amanda and I ask YeHoVaH to guide you into the fullness of His design. May you walk with Him in spirit and in truth all the days of your life.

A Call

Beloved, the Spirit of YeHoVaH is calling you now. The King is at the gate; His voice is clear, *"Remember My Sabbath day, to keep it holy."* It is not a burden but a gift, not a rule but a covenant of love. Today you stand at a crossroads, life or death, blessing or curse, obedience or rebellion. Do not harden your heart as generations before you did. If you have not kept the Sabbath, repent today. If you have treated it lightly, return today. The mercy of YeHoVaH is extended to you but His justice will not be mocked. You have heard the truth and now heaven calls you to respond. Will you enter His rest or will you stand outside when the gates are shut? The decision is yours. **Choose life, choose covenant and choose the eternal rest of YeHoVaH.**

Final Declaration

YeHoVaH, today I hear Your voice; I respond. I will no longer treat Your Sabbath as ordinary, nor will I walk in the empty ways of men. I repent and return to Your covenant sign You established from the beginning of creation. Father, write my name in the Lamb's Book of Life and let it also be found in Your Book of Remembrance, sealed by the blood of Yeshua. May I be counted among those who love Your appearing, who rejoice in Your rest and who embrace the gift of Shabbat with joy and holiness. With all my heart I declare, ***Come Yeshua, my Messiah and King.***

Reader Review: *"Isaiah 32:17-18 says that it's the work of righteousness that brings forth peace and the effect of righteousness is quietness and assurance forever. My people shall dwell in a peaceful habitation and a sure dwelling place. During creation God rested on the seventh day. We are to honor our Heavenly Father and enter into the sabbath as He did and rest. If we have unforgiveness in our heart towards anyone, our soul is restless; we can't enter into rest. Consider today any relationship where you're not at peace and ask your Heavenly Father to forgive you." By: Denise, Living Water Ministry*

Chapter 13
Shabbat: Heaven's Wedding Rehearsal

Shabbat is more than a rest day; it is a consecrated rhythm that YeHoVaH has built into the very heartbeat of creation. A rhythm that points us toward eternity. Week after week, Shabbat calls us to stop from our pleasures or normal everyday activities. We are to remember, prepare and rehearse for His set apart day. It is not merely a command to pause from labor but an instruction to enter into His covenant love, a rehearsal dinner before the greatest wedding feast in history, the marriage of the Lamb. Every candle lit, loaf broken and word spoken in prayer is part of heaven's rehearsal. Like the gentle flow of a stream that becomes a mighty river, Shabbat begins with childlike simplicity and deepens into profound spiritual mysteries as we learn to walk in its meaning.

Shabbat Is the Weekly Rehearsal of Covenant Love

YeHoVaH began with the simplest of instructions: *"**Remember the sabbath day, to keep it holy**"* (*Exodus 20:8*). This is like a child remembering a special day with a parent, a time set apart to be together. Shabbat is the weekly reminder that God loves His children. What He desires most from us is our time, attention and above all, our hearts.

But the word *"remember"* is not only about thinking; it is about acting. *"But be ye doers of the word, and not hearers only, deceiving your own selves"*(*James 1:22* KJV). As mentioned earlier in our book, the Hebrew word *zakar* means to remember in such a way that you do something about it. Just as a bride would never forget her wedding day, so we should never forget Shabbat. It becomes the anchor of our week, the covenant rehearsal of our love for YeHoVaH.

As we grow in understanding, we realize Shabbat is not about rules but about a relationship with the Father. Each week we renew our vows, saying with our actions and heart; *You are my GOD, and I am Your Bride.* Like a couple rehearsing for a wedding, we are training our hearts to live in covenant love that will one day be perfected at the marriage supper of the Lamb.

The Bridegroom Prepares a Table

Every week a table is set with bread, wine and candles. We speak blessings over spouses and children while fellowshipping with one another. All of it whispers of a greater table yet to come. For a child, it feels like a party. For the believer, it becomes a prophetic signpost. **Psalm 23:5** declares: *"Thou preparest a table before me…"* and **Revelation 19:9** promises: *"Blessed are they which are called unto the marriage supper of the Lamb."*

When we sit at the Shabbat table, we are not simply eating dinner; we are dining in rehearsal for eternity. The bread reminds us of Yeshua's body, the wine of His covenant blood and the fellowship of His united Bride. Our table becomes a reflection of the heavenly table that Yeshua the Messiah Himself is preparing for us.

The Shabbat meal is heaven's shadow on earth. *"Who serve unto the example and shadow of heavenly things…"* (**Hebrews 8:5** KJV). Just as a groom prepares a feast for his bride, Yeshua prepares an eternal banquet. Each time we eat and bless in His name, we taste eternity in advance.

The Bride Prepares Herself

If the Groom is preparing a feast, the Bride must prepare her heart. Scripture says: *"The marriage of the Lamb is come, and his wife hath made herself ready"* (**Revelation 19:7** KJV).

A child can understand the simplicity of preparation for a party. You just simply wash, dress and prepare. Shabbat is the rehearsal of a royal banquet, a joyful preparation not for a day alone but for the coming of the King.

As we mature, we understand that Shabbat is not only outward but inward preparation. It is the time to cleanse our hearts with prayer, renew our minds with His Word and clothe ourselves with His glory. It is a bridal training rehearsal.

At its deepest level, Shabbat is a rehearsal of sanctification. Each week, as Esther prepared for her king with oil and fragrance, we prepare for our King with purity and honor. Every Sabbath is one step closer to being ready for Yeshua's coming.

The Oil of Readiness

In **Matthew 25**, Yeshua told of the ten virgins. Five were wise because they carried oil; they were prepared. Five were foolish because they did not prepare; their oil ran out for use of other things they considered more important. Oil is a picture of readiness and the Spirit's filling. *"Let your loins be girded about, and your lights burning; And ye yourselves like unto men that wait for their lord, when he will return from the wedding; that when he cometh and knocketh, they may open unto him immediately"*
(**Luke 12:35-36** KJV).

When a child forgets to charge their flashlight, it won't give light when the darkness comes. In the same way, we need to stay filled with YeHoVaH's light so we can shine too. For us, Shabbat is the weekly recharge, renewal. It fills us with the oil of the Spirit, keeping our lamps burning brightly.

For the mature, this truth cuts deeper. Without Shabbat, our lamps begin to dim. Without the weekly filling of His Spirit, we risk falling asleep spiritually. The wise guard Shabbat because they know it is heaven's system for keeping the oil full, ourselves renewed and accountable.

Every Sabbath is a chance to trim our lamps, refill our vessels and ensure we are ready for the midnight cry: *"Behold, the bridegroom cometh!"*

Shabbat Announces His Kingship

Every wedding has vows spoken before witnesses. Shabbat is our weekly vow before heaven and earth. We stop our work and honor YeHoVaH's day. We proclaim that Yeshua the Messiah is King not only of our soul but also of our time, labor and family.

A child can simply declare: *"Yeshua is my King."* For the believer, it is the declaration that no other master such as money, business or culture rules our lives. For the mature, it is a radical act of loyalty. Every Sabbath we proclaim Yeshua is my:

- Messiah, not the world
- King, not my schedule
- Bridegroom, not my distractions

"A virtuous woman is a crown to her husband: but she that maketh ashamed is as rottenness in his bones." (***Proverbs 12:4*** KJV).

Just as a virtuous wife is the crown upon her husband, the Bride of Christ is called to be the crown for her Bridegroom. At the deepest level, her honor of the Sabbath itself is a crown laid at His feet, declaring Yeshua the Messiah is enthroned now and forever. Every time we honor His Sabbath, we proclaim to the universe that He reigns.

One day we will lay our crowns before Him (***Revelation 4:10-11***), offering back the fruit of our lives. Could it be that these crowns are the works that have been tested and refined by fire (***1 Corinthians 3:13***), the things that endure as eternal treasures? Just as Ruth laid herself at the feet of Boaz, we too will present ourselves before Yeshua, our Redeemer.

Every word spoken, every act of love, every work done in His name will be weighed. That which is false or self-serving will be consumed but what is pure will remain as an everlasting testimony to the King of the Universe. This is why the Bride must make herself ready (***Revelation 19:7***). When our works are tried by fire, may what remains be a crown of glory laid at His feet, our lives proclaiming that He alone is worthy.

A Rehearsal Means There Will Be a Wedding

No one rehearses for an event that will never come. The very existence of Shabbat proves the wedding is real. ***Hebrews 4:9*** declares: *"There remaineth therefore a rest [Shabbat-keeping] to the people of God."*

The teacher instructs their students to practice for the school play because the real performance is soon approaching. YeHoVaH would never give us weekly rehearsals if the eternal wedding feast were not guaranteed.

For the mature, this is the down payment of eternity. Each Shabbat is a deposit of the eternal rest, a guarantee of the kingdom to come. Keeping Shabbat is to live with expectation, anchoring our souls in the certainty that the Bridegroom will appear.

The Bridegroom Is Coming

Finally, Shabbat teaches us to listen. Yeshua said: *"And at midnight, there was a cry made, Behold, the bridegroom comes; go out to meet him"* (*Matthew 25:6* MBB).

The virtuous woman prepares her home with wisdom and care. She shapes her children's hearts to honor, their ears to listen and their steps to obey. Even as the father returns at the end of the day, she is attentive hearing the sound of the car in the driveway, gathering the children and readying them to run out and meet him with joy. In the same way, Shabbat trains our ears to listen for the coming of our King. Just as a mother teaches her children to listen for their father's return, we are called to teach our families to listen for the voice of our soon-coming Bridegroom. Each week, Shabbat becomes a rehearsal, shaping our hearts to be ready, attentive and eager for His appearing just as the feasts do.

For the believer, it is a discipline of tuning out the world's noise. For the mature, it is a prophetic training in hearing heaven. Every Sabbath silences the world's chaos so we can hear the whisper of eternity. When the final trumpet sounds [*Tekiah Gedolah*], only those who have rehearsed weekly will recognize it. Shabbat has been preparing us to rise, go out and meet our Bridegroom.

What We Look Forward to Every Shabbat:

- A meal that points to the Wedding Supper of the Lamb
- Candles lit to remind us of the wise virgins whose lamps were burning
- Rest that reflects the eternal rest in His Coming Kingdom
- The Sabbath we keep is saying, *"I am the bride who remembers. I am preparing for my Groom."*

In Conclusion

Sabbath is not just a pause in the week; it is heaven's weekly wedding rehearsal. It teaches us covenant love, sets a table of fellowship and purifies us as a bride. It also fills us with oil, proclaims His kingship, assures us of the coming wedding and trains our ears to hear the cry of the Bridegroom.

Every Sabbath is one more step closer to eternity. Every candle lit before sunset is a reminder of the virgins who kept their lamps burning. Every piece of bread broken reminds us of Yeshua's body given for our healing and wholeness and offers a foretaste of the eternal feast to come. Every cup of wine lifted is a testimony of the New Covenant in Yeshua's blood sealing us to Him forever. Every rest taken is a rehearsal for the eternal rest in His Kingdom.

Shabbat declares through the ages, **"The Bridegroom is coming! Prepare, Rehearse, Remember and Rejoice!"**

Chapter 14
Covenant Practices and Explanations

Sabbath is a rhythm of life, a sacred gift from YeHoVaH that draws us closer to His presence. Within its practices, we find both the heartbeat of Israel's faith and the testimony of Yeshua the Messiah, who fulfilled and deepened every commandment with His life. When fully entering the beauty of Sabbath, we rest from our labors. We also embrace the words, prayers and blessings that have shaped generations of believers. These practices are not merely traditions; they are living proclamations of faith that carry both prophetic meaning and personal transformation for every follower of Yeshua.

The Shema: Heartbeat of Faith

"Hear, O Israel: [YeHoVaH] the LORD our God, [YeHoVaH] the LORD is one! You shall love [YeHoVaH] the LORD your God with all your heart, with all your soul, and with all your strength" (**Deuteronomy 6:4-5**).

The word Shema in Hebrew means "hear" but it also carries the deeper meaning of obey, respond and act upon what you hear. When we recite the Shema, we are declaring, *"I hear You, [YeHoVaH] LORD and I will live according to Your truth."*

This declaration is both a prayer and a covenant response, an invitation to love YeHoVaH with our whole being. Yeshua Himself affirmed the Shema as the greatest commandment, embodying it perfectly in His obedience to the Father and His sacrificial love for humanity. From the daily reciting of the Shema to the blessing of bread and wine, each act connects us not only to ancient Israel but also to the living Messiah, the Bread of Life and the Cup of the New Covenant.

As we explore the Shema, the biblical order of the Last Supper and the Hebrew blessings spoken throughout Shabbat, we discover a sacred pattern designed to align our homes, families and hearts with the kingdom of God. These practices bring heaven's order into our daily lives teaching us to listen, obey and walk in covenant faithfulness. Whether through proclaiming the Shema, partaking of bread and cup in remembrance of Yeshua or speaking blessings over our family, each element draws us deeper into the eternal rhythm of worship, obedience and rest.

In the Life of Yeshua

When Yeshua was asked which commandment was the greatest, He quoted directly from the Shema: *"You shall love [YeHoVaH] the Lord your God with all your heart and with all your soul and with all your mind"* (***Matthew 22:37*** ESV). Yeshua did not just quote the Shema; He lived it. He obeyed the Father perfectly, taught His disciples to pray continually and sealed the covenant in His blood so the Torah could be written on our hearts (***Jeremiah 31:33***).

When to Recite the Shema

Traditionally, the Shema is spoken:

- In the morning upon rising
- At night before sleeping
- During Shabbat prayers
- During Appointed Feast Days
- In times of fear, war or uncertainty
- Before death or martyrdom

As believers, we recite the Shema with the full understanding that YeHoVaH is One and that our Redeemer Yeshua is the perfect expression of that unity.

Bringing the Shema into the Home

- Place it on your doorpost (*mezuzah*) as commanded
- Recite it with your children
- Let it be the first and last words on your lips each day

Bread and Cup: The Order of the New Covenant

At the Last Supper, Yeshua gave us a consecrated pattern to follow in remembering His sacrifice, first the bread and then the cup: *"And He took bread, and gave thanks, and brake it, and gave unto them, saying, This is My body which is given for you: this do in remembrance of Me. Likewise also the cup after supper, saying, This cup is the new [covenant] testament in My blood, which is shed for you"* (**Luke 22:19-20**).

Why Bread Comes First:

- **Symbol of Sacrifice:** The bread represents Yeshua's body, which had to be broken before His blood could be poured out. He was beaten, pierced and crucified; only through His death did His blood flow as the atonement for our sins. The bread comes first because the body is what carries the blood reminding us that His sacrifice was complete, both in flesh and in spirit.
- **Order of Covenant:** In Jewish tradition, when a covenant meal is shared, bread often begins the blessing. Yeshua honored this order and then deepened its meaning by adding the cup afterward.

- **Spiritual Pattern:** The bread reminds us that Yeshua is the *"Bread of Life"* (***John 6:35***). We first receive His life (*the Word made flesh*) and then we drink of His blood, which is the covenant seal of forgiveness (***Hebrews 9:22***).

Why Some Reverse the Order
Some Christian traditions begin with the cup, emphasizing the atonement in the blood. While sincere, this reverses the biblical sequence shown by Yeshua.

Correct Biblical Order
First the Bread, because His body was broken for us. Then the Cup, because His blood was shed for us. This order reflects not only the Gospel accounts but also the prophetic pattern of His sacrifice.

Hebrew Blessings: Words of Life

"From the rising of the sun to its setting The name of [YeHoVaH] the LORD is to be praised [with awe-inspired reverence]" (***Psalm 113:3*** AMP).

Shabbat is filled with timeless blessings that echo across generations. These are not empty rituals but powerful declarations of faith and thanksgiving that connect us with our covenant identity in YeHoVaH.

Common Blessings & Pronunciations

- *Baruch* (bah-ROOKH) - Blessed
- *YeHoVaH* (Yud-Hey-Vah-Hey) - LORD, ADONAI, HaShem
- *Eloheinu* (eh-lo-HAY-noo) - Our God

- *Melech ha'olam* (MEH-lekh hah-oh-LAHM) - King of the Universe
- *Kiddush* (kee-DOOSH) - Sanctification
- *HaMotzi* (hah-MOHT-see) - Blessing over bread

Family Application
Encourage children to learn one line each week. As they repeat and internalize the blessings, these words become part of their spiritual DNA.

Sabbath vs. Sunday: Timeline of Change

This timeline shows the biblical foundation of the Sabbath as YeHoVaH's covenant sign and how over time human traditions shifted worship to Sunday. It helps us discern whether today's church model reflects the Father's original plan or a corruption introduced by man.

Creation - *Genesis 2:2-3* God sanctified the seventh day as holy.
Exodus - *Exodus 20:8-11; 31:13* Sabbath was given as a covenant sign forever.
1st Century - *Acts 13, 17, 18* Believers, both Jew and Gentile, kept Sabbath.
2nd Century - Shift begins - Some Christians honor Sunday as the resurrection day, alongside the Sabbath.
321 A.D. - Constantine decrees Sunday as the empire's official rest day.
364 A.D. - Council of Laodicea forbids Christians from keeping Sabbath rest.
500 -1500 A.D. - Church grows in power as Sunday is solidified; cathedrals and wealth rise.
1500s - Reformation restores many truths but most Reformers keep Sunday worship.
1700s -Today - Modern churches continue Sunday traditions,

often tied to business and institutions.
Today - Messianic and Hebraic believers rediscover the truth of Sabbath.

Why We Do What We Do

The practices of Shabbat are not just rituals but living testimonies of our covenant with YeHoVaH. Every prayer, blessing and custom connects us back to the story of creation, when God rested on the seventh day and declared it sacred, a personal invitation. By setting apart this day, we declare with our lives that YeHoVaH is our Creator, Redeemer and King. Shabbat becomes a weekly reminder that our identity is rooted in Him, not in the chaos of this world.

When we light the candles, break the bread and lift the cup, we are not simply repeating tradition, we are entering into a rhythm of remembrance (*not forgotten*). The bread is a reminder of Yeshua's body, broken for us and the cup testifies of His blood, poured out for the remission of our sins. This sacred pattern teaches us that true rest comes only through His sacrifice and resurrection. In this way, every Shabbat meal becomes both a table of fellowship and a prophetic rehearsal of the marriage supper of the Lamb.

The reciting of the Shema is another central practice, declaring the oneness of God and our call to love Him with all of our heart, soul and strength. Speaking these words unite us with generations of believers before us who lifted their voices in loyalty and love for King of the Universe. For believers, the Shema is fulfilled in Yeshua the Messiah, who perfectly obeyed the Father and invited us into that same covenant relationship. We teach our children these words and engrave them in our homes to secure a legacy of faith that endures the test of time.

Blessings over the food and wine are more than polite prayers; they are affirmations that YeHoVaH is the source of every provision. Each blessing sanctifies the ordinary, reminding us that even eating and drinking can glorify God when received with thanksgiving. Learning to recite these Hebrew blessings connects us with the language of our ancestors and it is the Father's love language. Also, it invites God's presence more deeply into our homes. Over time, these blessings shape our hearts to see everything as a gift from above.

Musical Link Tips:

We have included a QR code to help make Sabbath meaningful for every generation. Scan it to access our webpage. This will allow you to view our YouTube channel and make a playlist of your favorite Sabbath songs. Cumbee's Worship songs and melodies stir the heart and create an atmosphere of peace, joy and reverence. Teaching children to sing, recite and actively participate ensures that they grow up not only knowing about YeHoVaH but experiencing His presence. In this way, the practices of Sabbath are not heavy burdens but life-giving rhythms that anchor us in God's rest and draw us closer to Yeshua, our eternal Sabbath rest.

Chapter 15
52-Week Torah Reading Cycle with Prophets & New Covenant Parallels

This chapter is designed to help you grow deeper in your walk with YeHoVaH week by week. Each portion (*Parashah*) begins with the Torah, is reinforced by the Prophets (*Haftarah*) and finds fulfillment in the New Covenant writings. As you read, you will notice that the Hebrew names of each portion are given alongside the English. This is intentional. It connects us to the ancient faith of Israel. It also helps us grow in understanding the language, culture and heart of Scripture as it was first given.

Approach each week's readings prayerfully, asking Ruach HaKodesh (*Set Apart Spirit, The Holy Spirit*) to open your eyes to the parallels and prophetic keys that connect the Torah, the Prophets and the New Covenant. The beauty of this cycle is that it repeats every year. This means as you walk through it once, you build a foundation and when you go through it again the next year, YeHoVaH will reveal even deeper treasures you may not have seen before. Year after year, the Torah cycle becomes a journey of discovery unveiling the character of our Father YeHoVaH, the salvation of His Son Yeshua and the guiding presence of Ruach HaKodesh (*Set Apart Spirit, The Holy Spirit*).

As you follow along, remember this is not just about gaining knowledge but about relationship and transformation. Each reading is an invitation to walk closer with Him, live out His commandments and discover how all Scriptures testify of the Messiah. Over time, you will see how every word points back to His covenant love and your heart will be strengthened in faith, hope and obedience.

How to Use This Chart

During a Jewish leap year, there are 54 parashot ha-shavua (*weekly Torah portions*) when an extra thirteenth lunar month is added to the calendar. In a regular year with only twelve months, there are fewer Sabbaths. So on certain weeks two parashot are combined and read together. In the chart, these combined portions are marked with "**RT** (*Read Together*)."

The annual Torah cycle concludes after The Feast of Tabernacles. On the eighth day, Shemini Atzeret, there is a holy gathering (***Leviticus 23:36***) and the final portion of ***Deuteronomy*** (*Parashah #54*) is read. The Torah scroll is rolled back to the beginning; the cycle immediately restarts with ***Genesis 1:1*** (*Parashah #1*). In this way, the Torah is read in full every year beginning and ending with great rejoicing.

In addition to the weekly readings, there are special Torah and Haftarah portions for YeHoVaH's feasts. These follow the rhythm of His calendar which begins in the fall with Yom Teruah. The readings listed here reflect the Diaspora tradition where certain feasts are observed for an extra day. This practice arose in ancient times when the new month was declared by sighting the crescent moon in Jerusalem; word of the sighting could not reach distant communities quickly.

To use this chart, simply follow the Torah portion listed for each week; beginning with Genesis and continuing through the Torah. After reading the Torah, turn to the Haftarah (*Prophets*) and then to the New Covenant passages to see how YeHoVaH weaves His Word together. Each portion includes its Hebrew name alongside the English. Take time to learn and remember them as part of reconnecting to the roots of your faith. As you read, ask Ruach HaKodesh (*Set-Apart*

Spirit, The Holy Spirit) to reveal the prophetic connections between the Torah, the Prophets and the New Covenant. When you complete the final week, begin again. Each yearly cycle opens fresh revelation of *YeHoVaH, Yeshua the Messiah and Ruach HaKodesh*.

Why Two Torah Portions Are Sometimes Read Together

While the Torah is divided into 54 portions, not every year contains enough Sabbaths to read each one individually. In a regular year with only twelve months, there are fewer Sabbaths than in a leap year. To keep the cycle complete, some portions must be read together on the same Sabbath.

This practice is also connected to the rhythm of YeHoVaH's appointed times (*Leviticus 23*). All of YeHoVaH's feast days that are designated as "a Sabbath of rest" are considered **High Sabbaths.** When a feast day (appointed time) coincides with the weekly Sabbath, the feast's designation takes precedence. This means the Torah reading, worship and prayers follow the feast day rather than the ordinary weekly Sabbath cycle. For example, if the first day of Unleavened Bread falls on a Sabbath, you would read the Torah portion for the feast rather than the standard weekly parashah.

The solution is to join two Torah portions on a later Sabbath. This ensures that the cycle remains aligned and always finishes on the eighth day. Deuteronomy is completed. The scroll is rolled back as the new cycle begins again with Genesis.

This system reflects the perfect order of YeHoVaH's calendar, where the weekly Sabbath and His appointed feasts interweave seamlessly into a unified rhythm of worship and remembrance.

52-Week Parashah Cycle

Week	Hebrew Meaning	English Meaning	Torah Reading	Haftarah (Prophets)	New Covenant
1	Bereshit	Beginning	Genesis 1:1-6:8	Isaiah 42:5-43:10	John 1:1-18; Hebrews 1:1-3
2	Noach	Noah	Genesis 6:9-11:32	Isaiah 54:1-55:5	Matthew 24:36-44; Luke 17:20-37
3	Lech Lecha	Go Forth	Genesis 12:1-17:27	Isaiah 40:27-41:16	John 8:51-58; Hebrews 7:1-19
4	Vayera	And He Appeared	Genesis 18:1-22:24	2 Kings 4:1-37	Luke 17:26-37; Hebrews 6:13-20
5	Chayei Sarah	Life of Sarah	Genesis 23:1-25:18	1 Kings 1:1-31	Matthew 8:19-22; John 4:3-14
6	Toldot	Generations	Genesis 25:19-28:9	Malachi 1:1-2:7	Matthew 10:21-38; Romans 9:6-16
7	Vayetze	And He Went Out	Genesis 28:10-32:3	Hosea 12:13-14:10	John 1:43-51
8	Vayishlach	And He Sent	Genesis 32:4-36:43	Obadiah 1:1-21	Matthew 2:13-23; Revelation 7:1-12
9	Vayeshev	And He Settled	Genesis 37:1-40:23	Amos 2:6-3:8; Zechariah 2:14-4:7	John 10:22-28; Acts 7:9-16
10	Miketz	At the End	Genesis 41:1-44:17	1 Kings 3:15-4:1	Luke 24:13-29
11	Vayigash	And He Approached	Genesis 44:18-47:27	Ezekiel 37:15-28	Luke 24:13-48
12	Vayechi	And He Lived	Genesis 47:28-50:26	1 Kings 2:1-12	John 13:1-19; Hebrews 11:21-22
13	Shemot	Names	Exodus 1:1-6:1	Isaiah 27:6-28:13; 29:22-23	Matthew 2:1-12; Hebrews 11:23-26
14	Va'eira	I Appeared	Exodus 6:2-9:35	Ezekiel 28:25-29:21	Luke 11:14-22; Romans 9:14-17
15	Bo	Come	Exodus 10:1-13:16	Jeremiah 46:13-28	Luke 2:22-24; John 19:31-37

16	Beshalach	When He Sent	Exodus 13:17-17:16	Judges 4:4-5:31	Matthew 14:22-23; Revelation 15:1-4
17	Yitro	Jethro	Exodus 18:1-20:23	Isaiah 6:1-7:6; 9:6-7	Matthew 19:16-30; Hebrew 12:18-29
18	Mishpatim	Judgments	Exodus 21:1-24:18	Jeremiah 34:8-22; Isaiah 66:1-24	Matthew 17:22-27; Hebrews 9:15-22
19	Terumah	Heave Offering	Exodus 25:1-27:19	1 Kings 5:12-6:13	Mark 12:35-44; Hebrews 8:1-6
20	Tetzaveh	You Shall Command	Exodus 27:20-30:10	Ezekiel 43:10-27	Matthew 5:13-20; Philippians 4:10-20
21	Ki Tisa	When You Take	Exodus 30:11-34:35	1 Kings 18:1-39	Mark 9:1-10; Acts 7:35-8:1
22	Vayakhel [RT with 23]	And He Assembled	Exodus 35:1-38:20	1 Kings 7:40-50	Luke 16:1-13; Hebrews 9:1-14
23	Pekudei [RT with 22]	Accounts	Exodus 38:21-40:38	1 Kings 7:51-8:21	Luke 22:1-13; Revelation 15:5-8
24	Vayikra	And He Called	Leviticus 1:1-5:26	Isaiah 43:21-44:23	Matthew 5:23-30; Hebrews 10:1-14
25	Tzav	Command	Leviticus 6:1-8:36	Jeremiah 7:21-8:3; 9:22-23	Mark 12:28-34; Romans 12:1-2
26	Shemini	Eighth	Leviticus 9:1-11:47	2 Samuel 6:1-7:17	Matthew 3:11-17; 2 Corinthians 6:14-7:1
27	Tazria [RT with 28]	She Will Conceive	Leviticus 12:1-13:59	2 Kings 4:42-5:19	Luke 2:22-35; Mark 1:35-45
28	Metzora [RT with 27]	Leper	Leviticus 14:1-15:33	2 Kings 7:3-20	Matthew 9:20-26; Hebrews 13:4
29	Acharei Mot [RT with 30]	After the Death	Leviticus 16:1-18:30	Ezekiel 22:1-19	Matthew 15:10-20; Hebrews 7:23-10:25
30	Kedoshim [RT with 29]	Holy Ones	Leviticus 19:1-20:27	Amos 9:7-15	Luke 17:1-10; 1 Peter 1:13-21

#	Name	Translation	Torah	Prophets	New Testament
31	Emor	Speak (Say)	Leviticus 21:1-24:23	Ezekiel 44:15-31	Matthew 26:59-66
32	Behar [RT with 33]	On the Mountain	Leviticus 25:1-26:2	Jeremiah 32:6-27	Luke 4:14-22
33	Bechukotai [RT with 32]	In My Statues	Leviticus 26:3-27:34	Jeremiah 16:19-17:14	Matthew 16:19-28; John 14:15-21
34	Bamidbar	In the Wilderness	Numbers 1:1-4:20	Hosea 1:10-2:22	Matthew 4:1-17; Luke 2:1-7
35	Nasso	Lift Up	Numbers 4:21-7:89	Judges 13:2-25	Luke 1:5-23; Acts 21:17-32
36	Beha'alotcha	When You Set Up	Numbers 8:1-12:16	Zechariah 2:14-4:7	Matthew 14:14-2; Hebrews 3:1-6
37	Shelach	Send	Numbers 13:1-15:41	Joshua 2:1-24	Matthew 10:1-14; Hebrews 3:7-19
38	Korach	Korah	Numbers 16:1-18:32	1 Samuel 11:14-12:22	John 19:1-17; Jude 1:1-25
39	Chukat [RT with 40]	Statute	Numbers 19:1-22:1	Judges 11:1-33	John 3:9-21, 19:38-42
40	Balak [RT with 39]	Balak	Numbers 22:2-25:9	Micah 5:6-6:8	Matthew 21:1-11; 2 Peter 2:1-22
41	Pinchas	Phinehas	Numbers 25:10-30:1	1 Kings 18:46-19:21	Mark 11:12-25; John 2:13-22
42	Matot [RT with 43]	Tribes	Numbers 30:2-32:42	Jeremiah 1:1-2:3	Matthew 5:33-37; Mark 11:12-25
43	Masei [RT with 42]	Journeys	Numbers 33:1-36:13	Jeremiah 2:4-28; 3:4	Mark 9:40-50; James 4:1-12
44	Devarim	Words	Deuteronomy 1:1-3:22	Isaiah 1:1-27	Matthew 24:1-22; John 15:1-16
45	Va'etchanan	I Pleaded (Ask for Mercy)	Deuteronomy 3:23-7:11	Isaiah 40:1-26	Luke 3:2-15; Romans 3:27-31
46	Eikev	Because	Deuteronomy 7:12-11:25	Isaiah 49:14-51:3	Matthew 16:13-20
47	Re'eh	See	Deuteronomy 11:26-16:17	Isaiah 54:11-55:5	John 6:35-51
48	Shoftim	Judges	Deuteronomy 16:18-21:9	Isaiah 51:12-52:12	John 14:9-20; Hebrews 10:28-31

49	Ki Tetze	When You Go Out	Deuteronomy 21:10-25:19	Isaiah 54:1-10	Matthew 24:29-42; Galatians 3:9-14
50	Ki Tavo	When You Come In	Deuteronomy 26:1-29:8	Isaiah 60:1-22	Matthew 4:13-24; Acts 28:17-31
51	Nitzavim [RT with 52]	Standing	Deuteronomy 29:9-30:20	Isaiah 61:10-63:9	John 12:41-50; Romans 9:30-10:13
52	Vayelech [RT with 51]	And He Went	Deuteronomy 31:1-30	Hosea 14:2-10; Micah 7:18-20; Joel 2:15-27	Hebrews 13:5-8
53	Haazinu	Listen	Deuteronomy 32:1-52	2 Samuel 22:1-51	Matthew 21:33-36; Hebrews 12:28-29
54	Vezot HaBracha	And This Is The Blessing	Deuteronomy 33:1-34:12	Joshua 1:1-18	Matthew 17:1-9; Jude 3-4, 8-10

The Blessings of Walking in the Whole Word

When you walk through the Torah, the Prophets and the New Covenant together, you are weaving the full tapestry of YeHoVaH's plan for your life. The Torah gives you foundation, like the strong roots of a tree. The Prophets lift your eyes to destiny, showing you YeHoVaH's promises and warnings across generations. The New Covenant brings the living fulfillment in Yeshua, who empowers you by His Ruach Kodesh (*Set Apart Spirit, Holy Spirit*) to live out everything the Word commands. This is not merely study; it is transformation. A child can grasp the stories but the wisest elder will still uncover mysteries that stir the soul.

Spiritually, this cycle nourishes your faith until it becomes unshakable. As you read the Torah, you discover YeHoVaH's holiness. When you absorb the Prophets, you gain courage to stand. As you embrace the New Covenant, you learn that YeHoVaH's power is made perfect in weakness. Over time, you will notice that temptations lose their hold, faith becomes easier and obedience feels like joy. You are not just reading; you are being changed into His likeness.

Physically, the Word teaches wisdom for life. Torah reveals YeHoVaH's order in food, health and rest. The Prophets show how obedience or rebellion affected nations, often in tangible, earthly ways. The New Covenant calls your body the Temple, reminding you that health is both stewardship and testimony. As you align with YeHoVah's rhythms, Sabbath rest, clean living and joyful feasts you will notice peace in your body and strength to endure.

Financially, YeHoVaH's Word is not silent. The Torah teaches principles of stewardship, generosity and cycles of blessing. The Prophets warn against greed and injustice while promising restoration for those who walk uprightly. The New Covenant declares that as you seek first the Kingdom of YeHoVaH's provision, opportunity and abundance will be added. Honoring His Word invites His blessing on the work of your hands because your labor is no longer just for survival but for the Kingdom's purpose.

This cycle ties your whole life to covenant relationship with YeHoVaH through Yeshua. Every week you are reminded that His promises are, *"Yes and Amen."* Every year you walk deeper into His love. The Torah shows you His ways, the Prophets anchor you in His promises and the New Covenant brings you face to face with His Son. If you will embrace this journey with humility and expectation, you will see growth beyond measure in spirit, health, provision and in destiny. The Word is living water and those who plant themselves by its streams will flourish in every season.

Chapter 16
Shabbat: The Covenant of the Bride

From the beginning of time, YeHoVaH has written His covenant into the rhythm of creation. On the seventh day, He rested, blessed it and set it apart as divine. That rest was not simply an end to labor; it was a personal invitation, the beginning of intimacy. It was the Bridegroom making space for His Bride, a weekly rehearsal of covenant love. Understanding Shabbat is to know the heartbeat of the Bridegroom for His people.

In the ancient Hebrew marriage customs, the path to covenant was clear. A bride was not taken lightly; she was chosen, valued and set apart. This process always began with the bride price. The groom (*or his father*) would pay a *mohar* (*bride price*) to prove the worth of the woman in his eyes. It was not a purchase but a declaration, *"You are priceless; I will sacrifice to have you."* Yeshua fulfilled this perfectly. At the Last Supper, He declared that His own blood would be the price of the covenant (**Matthew 26:28**), no silver, no gold, only His life poured out. As Peter wrote: *"Ye were not redeemed with corruptible things… but with the precious blood of [Yeshua] Christ"* (**1 Peter 1:18-19** KJV). Every Sabbath, when we cease striving and rest in Him, we remember that the Groom has already paid in full.

Once the bride price was shown, the next step was the cup of acceptance. A cup of wine was poured. The groom drank first and then he offered it to the bride. If she drank, she was saying, "*I belong to you.*" If she refused, the covenant was broken. In the same way, Yeshua lifted the cup at the Last Supper and offered it to His disciples: *"This cup is the new Covenant, ratified by my blood, which is being poured out for you"* (***Luke 22:20*** CJB). By drinking, they accepted the covenant, just as every believer does when they lift their cup in remembrance. Every Shabbat meal that includes the Kiddush cup is more than tradition; it is the Bride once again saying, *"Yes, my Beloved, I am Yours."*

When Yeshua prayed in the garden, He cried out, *"...O My Father, if it is possible, let this cup pass from me: nevertheless not as I will, but as you will"* (***Matthew 26:39*** MBB). That *"cup"* was the wrath of YeHoVaH poured out upon Him, wrath that we deserved, yet He bore. He knew there was no other way for redemption. Just as Abraham was willing to offer up his son Isaac, only to see YeHoVaH provide a ram in the thicket, so our Father revealed a greater mystery. When the time came for His own Son, His only begotten Son, there would be no substitution. Yeshua Himself was the Lamb provided. He was not spared, that we might be spared.

The Scriptures testify of His suffering: *"But he was wounded for our transgressions, he was bruised for our iniquities: the chastisement of our peace was upon him; and with his stripes we are healed"* (***Isaiah 53:5*** KJV). Though not a bone of His body was broken, His flesh was torn at the whipping post. His head was pierced by the crown of thorns, His hands and feet nailed to the tree and His side pierced by the soldier's spear. His body was shredded that we might receive healing; His blood was poured out that we might receive forgiveness.

Every time we take of the bread and the cup, we are remembering this covenant. The bread declares that by His stripes we are healed. The cup declares that by His blood we are forgiven. This is not a ritual to be done in vain but a holy act of remembrance. He gave His life for His Bride. The question remains; will you give your life to Him?

Beloved, as we prepare the table each Shabbat, let it not be with empty hands or divided hearts. Let us love Him more than the cares of this world. Let us tune our ears to hear the voice of our Savior and let us be ready for His return. For the Lamb who drank the cup of wrath is the same King who will soon drink the new cup with us in His Father's Kingdom.

This is why the Shabbat table is not ordinary. The bread, wine, blessing and fellowship mirrors the marriage supper of the Lamb (**Revelation 19:9**). Just as a groom prepares a feast for his bride, Yeshua is preparing the eternal banquet. Every time we break bread on Sabbath and drink from the cup, we are rehearsing for that day when heaven and earth will meet. Paul reminds us: *"For as often as ye eat this bread, and drink this cup, ye do shew [Yeshua's] the Lord's death till he come"* (**1 Corinthians 11:26** KJV). The Sabbath is not only a memorial of creation; it is a rehearsal of consummation.

The betrothal custom went even further. After the covenant cup was shared, the groom would leave his bride. He returned to his father's house to prepare a dwelling place. The bride did not know the day or the hour of his return. However, she lived every day in readiness, keeping herself pure, preparing her garments and listening for the sound of the trumpet that would announce his coming. Yeshua used this very imagery when He told His disciples: *"In my Father's house are many [rooms] mansions:... I go to prepare a place for you. And if I go... I will come again, and receive you unto myself..."* (**John 14:2-3** KJV).

The Sabbath and shofar join in power: *"He will send his angels with the sound of a great shofar. They will gather his chosen ones..."*(**Matthew 24:31** HTV). Yom Teruah, a High Sabbath, joins the power of the shofar and the rest of the Sabbath in a prophetic picture. The shofar shakes us from spiritual slumber, calling us to repentance and readiness, while the Sabbath rest positions us in holiness, consecration and trust in YeHoVaH's timing. Together they prepare the Bride to be awakened by the [*Tekiah Gedolah*] trumpet blast, resting in righteousness for the return of Yeshua and the great ingathering at His coming. Yom Teruah means *"Day of the Blast"* or *"Day of Shouting."* YeHoVaH commanded this day, in **Leviticus 23:23-25** and **Numbers 29:1,** as a holy [gathering] convocation and a memorial marked by the sounding of the shofar. It is not called a new year in the Torah; the very heartbeat is the trumpet. Later generations began to call this day Rosh Hashanah *"Head of the Year,"* marking the civil new year and the counting of kings. Yet, the essence of the day has never changed; it is the trumpet of YeHoVaH calling His people to awaken and shout. On this day, the shofar speaks in four voices:

- **Tekiah** - a clear blast proclaiming the King's reign
- **Shevarim** - three broken cries, the sob of repentance
- **Teruah** - nine urgent alarms, the cry of war and awakening
- **Tekiah Gedolah** - the great and final blast of victory

These rise together into 100 blasts, echoing through the heavens. In the days of Israel, when the Ark of the Covenant moved, the trumpet sounded (**Numbers 10:35-36**). It was the announcement that YeHoVaH was advancing, claiming ground and establishing His dominion. So, it will be again.

"It will take but a moment, the blink of an eye, at the final shofar. For the shofar will sound, and the dead will be raised to live forever, and we too will be changed" (**1 Corinthians 15:52** CJB).

Every weekly Shabbat is more than rest; it is a prophetic rhythm of time, a rehearsal for eternity. When the shofar sounds at the entrance of Sabbath, it is not just tradition; it is a declaration, ***"Our King is coming!"*** It proclaims to the enemy that his time is short; it reminds the Bride that her Bridegroom is approaching.

YeHoVaH's rhythm beats even deeper:

- **Shabbat** comes every week, a rhythm of rest and renewal
- **The Feasts** come each year, a rhythm of encounter and remembrance
- **The Shemitah** comes every seventh year, a rhythm of release, restoration and reset (*Leviticus 25:1-7*)

Together, these cycles are not empty rituals; they are prophetic training grounds. They tune our spirits to the calendar of heaven. They teach us to watch, wait and be ready. If we miss His timing, we may cling to our own holidays and traditions while overlooking the heavenly schedule. However, when we align with His appointed times, we step into the prophetic rehearsal of the great wedding day.

Childlike in its simplicity, yet profound in its depth, Shabbat weaves together covenant, communion and consummation. It teaches us to rest because He has paid the price. It invites us to drink because we belong to Him. It trains us to wait because He has gone to prepare a place. Yet it stirs us to listen for the last trumpet that will soon sound and the midnight cry that will call us to the greatest wedding feast of all.

Beloved, this is why Shabbat is not just a tradition or a day off. It is Heaven's wedding rehearsal. It is the Bride adorning herself, filling her lamp with oil, practicing the joy of rest and learning to hear the Bridegroom's voice.

Each week we are reminded:

- He has paid the price
- We have accepted the cup
- He is preparing the place
- He will return when the last trumpet sounds

As we close this journey, Amanda and I invite you to go even deeper in His Word. This book is only the beginning. Through our upcoming books, music, apparel bearing the Father's Name and worship resources, our heart's desire is to walk along with you as you prepare for the King.

At **Cumbees.com** you will discover not only teachings, devotionals and worship tools to help make your home a sacred dwelling of rest and preparation but also two life-giving companions to *The Gift of Shabbat*:

- **The Shabbat Guide:** This step-by-step manual is designed for each family member or guest at the Shabbat table to have their own copy. This way, everyone can participate, learn and even take one home to continue the celebration. Inside, you'll find the complete order of service, prayers, blessings and recipes for challah bread, along with ideas to make your home and table a place of beauty and joy. This guide equips you to share one of the greatest gifts our Father has given us, Shabbat. It will impact households and generations nationwide.
- **The Shabbat Journal:** This is a 52 Week Journey of Torah, Rest and Renewal. Each week provides you with the aligned portions of Scripture from the Torah, the Prophets and the New Covenant, woven together in harmony so you see the fullness of the Word as it was designed. Alongside these readings, you will find space to record your reflections, prayers and

testimonies. Over time, this journal becomes a treasure of remembrance, a living record of your walk with YeHoVaH and a legacy you can pass down for your children, family and those you mentor, ensuring your devotion continues as an inheritance of faith for generations to come.

We also offer **Covenant Decrees** that are more than words on a page; they are beautifully designed declarations of faith and identity. Each decree is a timeless artistry that includes a place to sign and date, marking your covenant commitment before YeHoVaH. Editions with witness signature lines are also available, allowing family and mentors to stand with you in agreement. Whether read in devotion, framed in your home or given as a gift, these decrees serve as both art and testimony, your covenant boldly written for all to see.

Alongside these resources, our **Apparel Collection** is more than clothing; it is a testimony you can wear. Each garment bears the Father's Name, expressing not only your personal faith but also serving as a visible light in a world of chaos. When someone asks about it, you have the opportunity to share the truth, the absolute truth of YeHoVaH and His Son, Yeshua. In this way, the apparel becomes both a shield of identity and a conversation of salvation.

Together, these books, decrees and garments are designed to help you build a lifestyle of remembrance, worship and preparation for His coming. They are treasures for your home, tools for your family and testimonies for the world.

Our vision does not end here. By the grace of YeHoVaH, we have already purchased land, brought in utilities, and begun excavation for a future House of Torah and Worship. Since parts of North Carolina have experienced flooding in the past, we will be raising the elevation of our future building site so that its foundation will be secure and protected from potential flooding in the years to come. This ensures that in times of natural disaster, this refuge will stand strong, a facility equipped to serve surrounding communities with food, resources and relief.

This House will also serve as a center of worship, where services can be livestreamed to the nations, youth can be mentored in truth and weekly messages of life and eternity can be broadcast to the world. It is our vision that friends and family from the nations may come and celebrate the appointed feast days with us, bringing their RVs, pitching their tents and gathering together as one people before the King. This is our future, a place where heaven looks down and sees the love of the Father poured out upon His people. If YeHoVaH stirs your heart, we would greatly appreciate your prayers and support in helping us prepare this site and raise this structure, so His light can shine even brighter. Together, we can build a place of worship, restoration and preparation. It will be a home for His presence and a refuge for His people. Come be part of YeHoVaH's family at **CUMBEES House of Torah and Worship** and let us walk with you as you journey deeper into covenant, clothed in identity and prepared as the Bride for the King.

Now, let us return to where it all began, the gift of rest. The greatest treasure we have been given is not only the promise of heaven but the presence of the King here and now. Resting in Him is to live as His Bride, prepared, adorned and waiting for His return. Just as Esther prepared herself before her king, may you also make ready your heart before the King of Kings. Like the wise virgins, may you keep your lamp full of oil and your faith burning brightly. May each Sabbath draw you deeper into YeHoVaH's rest and prepare your heart for the return of the Bridegroom, Yeshua the Messiah.

A Personal Request from Scott & Amanda Cumbee

Dear Friend,

We pray that this book has stirred your heart, deepened your faith and helped you draw closer to Yehovah's eternal covenant of rest. Our desire is not only to share this truth with you but to see it spread far and wide so that countless others can also discover the blessing and restoration found in Shabbat.

One of the most powerful ways you can help us accomplish this is by leaving a review on Amazon. Every review, even just a few heartfelt sentences, becomes a voice that tells the world this message matters. Reviews don't just help a book rank higher; they plant seeds that carry Yehovah's Word further than we ever could on our own.

Please Help Us Spread the Truth!
By leaving your review, you help unlock the gift of Shabbat for others who are searching for His eternal rest. Your words may be the very reason someone else decides to begin their journey into Yehovah's covenant of peace.

To leave your review go to your amazon page or simply:
Scan the QR code below with your phone's camera.

Thank you for standing with us, for sharing this message and for helping spread the light of His truth to the nations. May Yehovah richly bless you.

With Love and Gratitude,
Scott & Amanda Cumbee

www.ingramcontent.com/pod-product-compliance
Lightning Source LLC
Chambersburg PA
CBHW050517100526
44581CB00001B/6